The Leno Wit

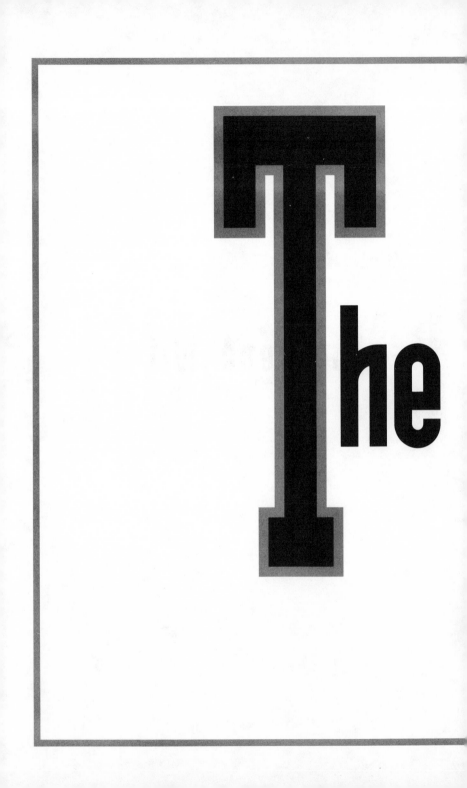

Leno Wit

His Life and Humor

BY JAY (William) WALKER

WILLIAM MORROW AND COMPANY, INC.
NEW YORK

It is the policy of William Morrow and Company, Inc., and its imprints and affiliates, recognizing the importance of preserving what has been written, to print the books we publish on acid-free paper, and we exert our best efforts to that end.

Library of Congress Cataloging-in-Publication Data

Walker, Jay (Jay William)
    The Leno wit : his life and humor / Jay Walker.
        p.   cm.
    ISBN 0-688-14993-6
    1. Leno, Jay. 2. Television personalities—United States—Biography. 3. Co-
    medians—United States—Biography.   I. Title.
PN1992.4.L382W36 1997
792.7'028'092
[B]—DC20   96-34269
                                                                  CIP

Printed in the United States of America

First Edition

1   2   3   4   5   6   7   8   9   10

BOOK DESIGN BY RENATO STANISIC

Contents

The Leno Wit

Gentle No More?

Gone are the garish metallic suits, the short black hair, and the one-dimensional stand-up comic of the early nineties.

These days Jay Leno is a snappy dresser with a pricey, tailored wardrobe that doesn't glitter, with a full head of grizzled hair, and with a comedy repertoire that goes well beyond his proven expertise of being able to perform a hilarious stand-up monologue off the top of his head.

And all for the better, especially his expanding funny-man repertoire, which now includes playing parts in skits à la Johnny Carson, though Leno's characters are pure Leno and bear little resemblance to such Carson skit personas as Carnac and Art Fern.

Leno has his own stock of funny characters, among them Iron Jay, whose technologically enhanced head, otherwise known in the trade as a "morphed" head, your basic fathead, a head that looks like nothing so much as a sumo wrestler, fills the TV screen and cracks wise. The giant head is so grotesque that it's funny.

To be sure, Leno has a large head to begin with, what with that lantern jaw that dominates his face, more or less caricaturing it by making it even bigger. And that strikes the funny bone in his legions of fans.

This was not always the case.

Early critics, noting Leno's prognathous jaw and rigid walk, likened him to Frankenstein's monster, who despite Jay's squeaky Mickey Mouse voice, struck fear in the hearts of his audience.

His outrageous looks were almost enough to deep-six his career in show biz even before he could get started. One Hollywood casting director, who shall remain nameless to protect his genetically inherited idiocy, had the effrontery to claim Leno's aspect "frightened" little children.

Leno's personality is and always has been anything but frightening. He is still the same Jay he was before he hit the big time when he assumed the helm of *The Tonight Show.* Some things never change, and for this his admirers are grateful.

Regarding those boxy metallic suits Leno wore when he was less than a clothes horse, he once explained that he had bought a ten years' supply from a door-to-door salesman. Maybe that salesman no longer makes house calls. In any case, those boxy numbers are definitely a thing of the past.

Standing six feet tall and weighing in at 180 pounds, Leno is an imposing presence. His kindly aquamarine eyes and ever-smiling mouth convey geniality, convincing those watching him that he is, if anything, an amiable hulk who wouldn't hurt a fly. In short, what you see is what you get.

It's David Letterman's considered opinion that there is only one difference between Leno onstage and Leno off: "Jay wears less makeup onstage."

That was Leno before he got the brass ring—i.e., *The Tonight Show*. He was fair game, and everyone was always criticizing him, with his wardrobe proving to be one of their favorite targets.

Not only his suits but his ties came in for derision. Said comedian Dennis Miller during his stint on *Saturday Night Live,* "Those ties look like they were made in summer camp, like fabric ashtrays he's wearing around his neck."

Letterman again: "I don't *get* his clothes. I just don't get it. I don't get the pushed-up sleeves, the luminescent ties."

His basic Fuller Brush–salesman attire simply never caught on for Leno. His friends made Leno's wardrobe sound like he was the guest of honor at a convention of Ringling Brothers' clowns, with the ties that squirt water or ink and with the baggy outfits.

It wasn't only fellow comedians who poked fun at Leno's garb. Get this dig by *People* correspondent Patti Corcoran: "Jay Leno has no—absolutely no—taste in clothes. It's not a minority opinion. Just ask his friends."

Even Leno's mother had a problem with his wardrobe. She often kidded him: "It's no wonder no one ever recognizes you on the street—you're always a mess!"

Associated Press's Dana Kennedy wrote that Leno's mother said of him: "He can't *wait* to get the tuxedos off! He likes to go off and fool around with his motorcycles."

At that time in his life, before his big break in television, Leno did not give a hang about the clothes he wore. All he cared about were his jokes. The only thing he knew about clothes was that "you really shouldn't show your genitals in public" (this according to a *Playboy* article about him).

When he was first trying out a career in comedy, Leno simply did not do impressions or play characters in skits. Playing a character was a form of typecasting as far as he was concerned.

He pointed out, "You're stuck with the thing. If you're the Wacky Guy from Space, you might get on Carson one or two times. But the third time, you're just a guy in a space suit telling jokes."

That was the reason he liked Laurel and Hardy so much as a kid—"because no matter where they were, they were always Laurel and Hardy. I mean, if you put them in the Renaissance or had them signing the Magna Carta, they were still Stan and Ollie. Their personalities were ingrained, and that made me laugh."

Leno always liked comics that looked like ordinary people, such as Jack Benny, Alan King, Johnny Carson, and Bob Newhart. He never went in for the put-on-a-dress school of comedy.

To top it all off, it's a much simpler matter to play just one character—to wit, yourself.

Leno is an honest product of American humor. Like American humor, his jokes fall into separate and distinct categories. One of these categories is derived from the old-fashioned "tall tale" as practiced in the West by the great Mark Twain; the other is the one-liner, as practiced by such comic luminaries as Henny Youngman: "Take my wife—please!"

When Leno started, he had no idea he would ever be constructing jokes, not only at a fast pace but every day of his life. Instead, he studied himself, and shaped his humorous style on the traditional anecdote, the tall tale in miniature. The one-liners were a much later product.

Even during the period when Leno appeared as a guest of Johnny Carson or David Letterman, he mined the anecdotal lode without shame. He had become a natural storyteller, probably having inherited the trait—or learned it—from his father, who was a professional salesman and later insurance manager.

"I'm always me," he said of his early career as a stand-up comic using no props at all. In 1992 he reminisced to Oprah Winfrey about his early days in show business before he got his start. In the following, note the absence of props, costumes, or other distractions in the carefully crafted anecdote, featuring nothing but Leno and the spoken word.

"I went to this strip joint, you know, and I went backstage, and I went to the guy's office, and there's a stripper with him, just as you would imagine.

"He goes, 'Yeah?'

"I say, 'I'm a comedian.'

" 'Comedian?'

"I say, 'And I want to work your club.'

" 'You in the union?'

"I say, 'No, I didn't know.'

" 'Well, you got to join the union you want to be a comedian. You can't work the union club, you can't work here unless you're in the union, you know.'

"I say, 'Oh. Well, how do I get in the union?'

"And he goes, 'Here, go see my buddy over there.' And he writes this address. He says, 'I'll call him up, tell him you're coming.'

"So I go across town, this guy's place, and knock on the door.

" 'Come in.'

" 'I'm Jay Leno, the guy—'

" 'Oh, yeah, yeah. You're a comedian. All right. How long you been a comedian?'

"I say, 'Oh, about a year.'

"He says, 'A year?' He goes, 'You got to join the union within six months. You could be in violation. I could fine you!' He starts yelling. I'm just—I'm like twenty years old. I'm scared, you know?

"I say, 'All right. How much is it to join the union?'

"He says, 'Five hundred dollars.'

"And I say, 'Five hundred?' I say, 'I don't have five hundred dollars.'

"And then he says, 'Well, how much *do* you have?'

"I went into my pocket and took out whatever I had. I had, like, seventy-five dollars. 'Well, I got—' And as I said it I knew I was being taken.

"He goes, 'What do you got? Seventy-five?' And he takes my seventy-five dollars, and he doesn't even put it in the drawer. He puts it in his pocket. And he writes 'union man' on a card, and he signs his name. He gives it to me. He goes, 'You just show this to anybody.'

"I say, 'Really? Okay, thank you.'

"So I went back to the place where I'd just been, right? And I knock on the door.

"The guy goes, 'You see my friend Larry?'

"I say, 'Yeah.'

" 'What did he give you?'

" 'He gave me a union card.'

"The guy laughs. 'You know, that guy—he's a killer! Kid, I don't need anybody now, but thanks anyway.'

"Oh, it was awful! But you know, you're just a kid. And you get taken—oh, oh."

In order to show the contrast between Leno's two styles of humor, take a look at a current example of a punchy, up-to-date, no-holds-barred one-liner from a recent stand-up routine. Incidentally, *one-liner* is a misnomer, as is evident here. Many one-liners actually are composed of three or even four sentences.

Leno, after Boris Yeltsin had just pinched two female assistants in October 1995 in full view of a television camera: "Those poor Russian people. They have a president with low popularity and no foreign policy and who can't keep his hands off women. Well, they wanted an American-style government, and they got it."

Things are different today for Jay Leno. As star of *The Tonight Show* he has changed his opinion about playing wacky characters and using props and other technological improvements in film and television. He has expanded his comedic routines to include the likes of Iron Jay, Larry the Lawyer, and Mr. Brain. His fans have voted their approval by tuning in his NBC show and increasing his ratings enough to outstrip Letterman's numbers on CBS.

A main reason Leno did not want to play a character other than himself was an experience he had early in his career. He broke his rule and cracked a joke that was in direct contrast to his nice-guy image—a joke about Bolivian Marching Powder.

He detailed to John McCollister of the *Saturday Evening Post* what happened when he changed his routine in even that small a fashion.

Leno and his comedian buddies were hanging around shooting the breeze when one of them told a joke about drugs. Everyone laughed—including Leno. The jokester advised Leno to "try that onstage."

"I don't do drug jokes," Leno protested.

"That's okay. Try it."

And so one night Leno changed his mind when his act onstage showed signs of faltering. He decided to regale his audience with the drug joke. The audience split its collective sides when he was through. Leno was taken aback. He had felt sure that the joke would die if he were to tell it, given his clean-cut image.

But that is not the end of the story. Later, a member of the audience came up to him after the show and asked, "What was this thing you did about drugs? That doesn't sound like you. Do you use drugs?"

Leno couldn't believe his ears. The only joke the guy remembered was the drug joke, the one joke in Leno's routine not written by Leno.

Right then and there Leno made up his mind never to do a joke that was out of character for him. His squeaky-clean image would not be tarnished for the sake of one measly joke.

"I'm the same guy onstage and off. All that stuff about 'laughing on the inside, crying on the outside'—I don't get it." Leno was so carried away at the time that he did not even get the aphorism right, but no matter. His point was clear.

Leno does not care for hostile jokes that may hurt someone's feelings. "More and more people are telling me how much they dislike the mean-spirited material of today's comics—the ethnic bashing, the woman bashing, the gay bashing—that was big for a while on TV. There will always be a place for dirty in comedy. When it's done right, funny is funny. No one is ever bothered by George Carlin's material. He's never mean-spirited."

Andrew Dice Clay is a horse of a different color, according to

Leno. Clay, the quintessential trash talker (who later cleaned up his act temporarily and starred in a sitcom that failed), has no place in comedy.

"Have you seen Andrew Dice Clay anywhere lately?" Leno had asked *TV Guide* back in 1991. "That concert film of his that Twentieth Century-Fox has decided not to release—it probably wasn't because of its dirt, but because it had no real jokes in it."

Mavis Leno, Jay's wife, was once asked if it was true that Jay was as nice as his image suggests.

She answered, "Jay is a man with an almost limitless amount of goodwill. That comes across onstage no matter what he's saying. Jay sees himself as just a regular guy."

Joe Six-Pack at your service.

In those early days, Leno felt that tinkering with his image and adding loony characters to his routine would detract from his jokes.

"I used to feel guilty when I walked onstage in Vegas and didn't have lights and lasers, but then people would come up and say how much they enjoyed just being talked to. People are so used to being lip-synched and teched out that they think it's amazing that people can do things by themselves. I think you need that communication. That's why I like comedy—it's real low-tech."

Perhaps that was true back then. It is equally true now that Leno experiments with the technological medium of television, for example, when he assumes his Mr. Brain or Iron Jay character on camera. Currently, he is unafraid to branch out in the art of comedy for these two characters and others he may come up with. As any artist worth his salt should, he makes use of the high technology at hand—in this case, cinematic technology.

After all, why should he limit himself to doing stand-up monologues for the medium of television when it allows so much more high-tech inventiveness than does a nightclub? He is willing to take risks in the name of his art. This is all to the good.

Being a nice guy doesn't mean Leno can't attack corporate America. "I would rather make fun of the corporation, or whatever it is that dehumanizes people, than make fun of people themselves. Nowadays you make fun of nuclear power, giant computers that send people nine-thousand-dollar phone bills; you laugh at that because here is a chance for the human spirit more or less to triumph over the machine. . . . It all comes down to good jokes. It all comes down to whether it's funny or not."

Not even McDonald's is safe from his joke factory. "McDonald's is hiring senior citizens. This must be part of their cradle-to-grave minimum-wage program. It's nice to know that when you're eighty you can make the exact same money you made when you were sixteen."

Some subjects are sacred cows for nice-guy Leno, and he steers clear of them.

"Comedy is supposed to be the underdog making fun of the big guy. I get annoyed when I see humor that is fascist or racist. Or misogynist or anti-Semitic. I defend people's right to say whatever they want. I just don't particularly care for it."

The joke's the thing, in other words. Not the hatred born of self-serving political factions.

"I wouldn't mind if there was a *joke* there." Instead of bile-spewing hate. "It's always funny to me how if you make fun of ethnic groups or make fun of women or something like that, then you're on the cutting edge, but if you go after our foreign policy or the savings-and-loan scandal or Washington, that's just like getting a Walt Disney *G* rating."

No wonder *Vanity Fair* dubbed him the "Mr. Clean of contemporary comedy."

It is Leno's contention that audiences don't want to listen to trash-talking comics.

"People yell at you in traffic and give you the finger," he told Lawrence Christon, correspondent for the *Los Angeles Times.* "You're running up against it all day long. You don't need to pay twenty dollars to hear a guy swear at you from the stage."

He refined his attitude a bit upon his position regarding smut in the following words: "Oh, a few people are successful with it, like Richard Pryor. But it's a moral thing. You see a grandfather and a little kid, you don't want to yell obscene words at them. I don't object to it in other comedians. I just don't do it."

Which fits hand in glove with Leno's image as the kindly gibester.

To protect his carefully crafted nice-guy image, Leno refuses to endorse certain products. "I don't drink, smoke cigarettes, or take drugs. I'm probably the straightest guy I know. So I'm not going to help sell beer or tobacco."

On the other hand, he has no compunction about participating in commercials for products that do not conflict with his image.

He told *Cosmopolitan* in 1989, "I agreed to do Doritos because it's a tasty chip and because I've never seen six dead teenagers on the highway with empty bags of Doritos around. It's not an inherently destructive product."

Beer is another story. "I won't do beer ads. I don't think these beer companies should be trying to get young adults—which we all know means teenagers—to drink beer. I don't want some father to come to my show saying, 'My kid got killed because of your ad.' I draw the line at taking money for something I don't use."

Waxing jingoistic, he defends his Doritos commercials. "I have no interest in selling products that aren't American-made. I don't perform in other countries; why should I sell their products? I intend to be very nationalistic when it comes to industrial America. Doritos are harmless. I mean, obviously, it's not an apple."

Leno has not changed his image over the years, despite his recent success on *The Tonight Show*.

Part and parcel of Leno's image is his belief in the work ethic. "I consider myself a good soldier. You go to work, you do the job—write joke, tell joke, get check—and the world will pretty much take care of itself."

Leno can't think of anything else he would rather do than work. "I love keeping busy, seeing things through. It's how I relax. People say, 'Oh, I'll bet you sit in your pool all day.' Well, I went and sat in my pool once and hated it. I felt like a leaf."

Leno is, as one pundit noted, the "working man's comedian," perhaps on account of his work ethic. Certainly he doesn't do his monologues in coveralls, gripping a monkey wrench. He has also been called the "thinking man's comedian"—this on account of his arsenal of sly political jokes.

Let's look at some of these. Politicians intrigue Leno because of the fact that humor is usually aimed at hypocrites and most politicians are hypocrites by the very nature of their work. Here's what Leno thought about Dan Quayle's statement that Colin Powell might not make a good president because when the going gets tough, Powell might be reluctant to take the offensive: "You all remember, when Powell was hiding in Vietnam, Quayle was bravely protecting the Dairy Queen in Bloomington, Indiana."

Leno, on the most frightening aspect of Halloween: "It's not the monsters or vampires. It's that week after Halloween, when your pumpkin dries out and starts to look like Strom Thurmond."

Actors get roughed up by his acerbic wit, too. Here's what Leno thought about Alec Baldwin's reported roughing up of a photographer: "A little Halloween tip for kids. If you were planning to trick or treat at Alec Baldwin's house, do not dress up as a photographer."

And President Clinton remains a beautiful target. When he requested the presence of Jane Fonda, Ted Turner, and the Atlanta Braves at the White House, Leno said: "That's a smart move because the president can learn a lot from them. . . . Ted can teach him how to put together a winning team, and Jane can tell him what it was like to go to Vietnam."

When someone came up with a book of *101 Lines Men Tell to Women,* Leno picked out this one as his favorite: "Yeah, *Bridges of Madison County* made me cry too."

In 1995, Quebec voted not to break away from the rest of Canada, and Leno noted: "It was agreed, however, that Quebec can start dating other countries."

And he doesn't really have too much respect for royalty, either. About Queen Elizabeth's first flight across the ocean on a commercial airline, he had this reaction from other passengers: "They said it was a pain. She spent the entire flight sitting on the throne, and nobody else could get in there."

On a United Airlines flight, an inebriated investment banker was busted after relieving himself on a service cart. Leno: "His lawyer is now trying to plea-bargain it down from a Number Two to a Number One."

One day a cougar cub bit House Speaker Newt Gingrich's chin. "Details on the story are sketchy," Leno said. "In fact, we can't even know which of Newt's chins he bit."

The Department of Agriculture decided to permit two pellets of rat fecal matter per two kilograms of breakfast cereal. "Do you know what the technical name for grain and fecal matter in food is? A *hot dog.*"

When news spread like wildfire that Chris Darden and Marcia Clark were to be married, Leno came up with this observation: "I hope they don't pick Judge Ito to do the ceremony. . . . He will limit them to one conjugal visit a week."

In general, it is his political savvy that makes Jay Leno one of the most talked-about and listened-to comedians in the business. For example: "Dole claims Clinton can't tell the difference between a lie and a joke. I think it's pretty easy to tell. A lie is a Democratic economic plan. A joke is the Republican economic plan."

Or how about this one? "You've seen the news—Bill Clinton in L.A., playing pickup basketball at a South Central playground? Now I know where they got the idea for the movie *White Men Can't Jump.*"

Or this semipolitical one? "Have you heard about the latest survey? A Gallup poll says 67 percent of Americans believe Michael Jackson when he says he didn't do anything. That's pretty good. How do you think that makes Bill Clinton feel? He's the president, and he's twenty points behind Michael Jackson in believability."

Or this astute observation: "Here's something: White House

economists announced yesterday the economy is slowing down. How do you slow down after four years of George Bush? What are we, in reverse?"

Sometimes his laughs are a bit tongue in cheek. "This is pretty amazing. Those suspects in the World Trade Center bombing—they reportedly were considering kidnapping Richard Nixon and Henry Kissinger for ransom. How stupid can you get? All they had to do was ask—we'd have given them to 'em."

Clinton never stays out of his sights for long. "Retroactive taxes, right? President Clinton wants to go back to January first, let everybody pay taxes all over again. I say, let's go back to November first and vote all over again."

He had this to say about Clinton at the Mideast peace-signing ceremony: "All the former presidents were there, saluted for their role in bringing about peace. Carter, of course, for the Camp David agreement. Bush for helping start the current talks, and Clinton for just staying out of the way."

But Leno's eyes are just as sharp looking over other names in the news. Here he zeroes in on a name not easily forgotten: "Another daytime talk show started recently. Tammy Faye Bakker [Messner] got her own program. You know, actually it's making television history. This is the first time the host of a show is more dysfunctional than any of the guests."

Or this celeb: "Hey, you know who got married? Olympic skater Tonya Harding. Yeah, actually, kind of an embarrassing moment for the groom. Did you see this on the news? I guess at the bachelor party, the stag film they showed was a video of her from her last honeymoon. The guy who proposed to her—that is one brave guy. That's the first time that anyone around Tonya has gotten down on one knee and been able to get up again!"

* * *

Leno did grow up in a rough-and-tumble, blue-collar, comfortably middle-class neighborhood. Even so, he wears a suit and tie at work every day. Not that Leno denies his blue-collar roots. In fact, he has nothing but fond memories of his childhood.

So what if Jerry Seinfeld ridicules him for dressing "like an Iranian disco owner." Leno's fans recognize him as just one of the guys in the neighborhood. Maybe the guy down the street with his old Dodge up on blocks. The guy you see tinkering with his car on the weekends.

2

One of the Guys

James Douglas Muir Leno was born on April 28, 1950, in New Rochelle, New York, the son of an Italian-American insurance salesman, Angelo Leno, and of a Scottish-born housewife, Cathryn Muir Leno.

Leno believed he would follow in his father's footsteps and become a salesman, which accounts for the Fuller Brush man image he seems to have developed as he grew up. He could have been a salesman—or a mechanic. Yet he never looked like a grease monkey, or anything resembling a garage guy. In the end, perhaps, that was the reason why he opted for the salesman image to cover his comedy career.

Nobody called Leno Jay until grade school. His family knew

him strictly as Jamie. His only brother, Patrick, was ten years older than he, went on to Yale, and made his living as a lawyer in insurance litigation. Still does, for that matter.

Leno's parents provided both their kids with an easy life. As a result, Jay grew up happy, with plenty to cheer about.

Occasionally he jokes about his middle-class upbringing. "I came from the kind of family where my mom ironed my socks. In case my shoe ever fell off, people would know I came from a good family."

Nevertheless, his mother, Cathryn Leno, once gave a spirited response to this teasing about her meticulousness. "In my day we always starched and ironed the men's shirts. And while your iron was hot, why wouldn't you also do the socks?"

At the age of nine, Jay packed up with his family and moved in 1959 to Andover, Massachusetts, where he spent what remained of his youth.

By all accounts he idolized his father. As Leno once said, "I just assumed I'd always be some sort of gregarious salesman who knew a joke to emcee birthday parties."

It was a good life. "I grew up in a house where the parents were adults. I saw them have fun, even act a little silly, but they never acted like children. And there was no yelling. I could never understand sitcoms where the husband and wife scream at each other. No one in my family was like that."

Leno's life was a flat-out ball at this time. He was so happy he wanted to spread his good cheer to those around him. Practical jokes were one way he had of accomplishing this feat. In junior high school he lit cherry bombs at urinals and, one-upping that prank, flushed tennis balls down toilets, watching toilet water inundate the floor tiles with glee.

That was nothing compared to his favorite prank of skulking into the ladies' room and pouring water into the Kotex dispenser. He confessed in 1986, "I liked watching that metal machine expand and tear apart from the napkins' absorbing the water. It was very funny. It would be a good ad for Kotex."

He noted: "But these were not career moves."

He looked the part of a comedian even as a toddler. His wife, Mavis, said of a baby picture of him, "His face is just popping with mischief. He had curly black hair and almond-shaped eyes. You can see that there is some kind of forceful personality just dying to emerge."

Leno remembers the day when his mother, chiding him as a kid, told him, "There's a time to be funny and a time to be serious," and of course he never could figure out when the time to be serious was. No one ever *said* when that would be.

With an attitude like that, Leno was bound to end up as a comedian. It was inevitable; it was fate.

His mother did not think so, though she admitted he was funny. "He was always funny, Jay was. He was always joking as a child. But we thought he was going to be a salesman like his father."

She was glad it took him a long time to become a show-biz success story. "It took him a while to get to where he is, but that was the way I wanted it. I didn't want him pushed, pushed, pushed." She meant she didn't want him to go up like a rocket, explode, and disappear into nothingness. She wanted his success, when it came, to be lasting.

Leno feels he inherited his striking chin and his blue eyes from his Scottish mother and his black hair and tawny complexion from his Italian father.

In 1985, Leno took his mother to Greenock, Scotland, the place of her birth. As Cathryn Leno took her son on a guided tour of the modest-sized town, she kept pointing at local Scotsmen who looked just like him. It was spooky. A whole town full of Jay Lenos!

As a kid Leno simply couldn't help being nice. Like his lantern jaw, it was in his genes to be decent.

Cathryn Leno bore this out. "He was always helpful, too. If a car was broken down on the road, he'd get out and help. He had such a happy disposition."

Thinking he was growing up to be a mechanic thanks to his penchant for cars, she told him that, "as an investment, he should buy a service station. That way he'd have plenty of room to store more cars. What's he got out there in Beverly Hills? Twenty cars?"

Actually, at this point Leno owns thirty cars.

According to his mother, only one thing ever truly ticked Leno off. "The only time I ever saw Jay get mad was over his car, if anybody borrowed his car. He's got all those cars out there now, but *we* can't drive them."

On a pleasure trip to Beverly Hills to visit Leno, she asked him if she could use one of his cars to get around.

Leno said, "Mother, I'll *rent* you a car."

When Leno repaid the compliment with a visit to his parents at the old neighborhood, he recalled, "I went to see a guy I grew up with, and his mom actually said to me, 'Well, what are you going to do when this show business thing slows down? You going to come back our way?' "

Flabbergasted, Leno commented, "I mean, I'm the host of *The Tonight Show,* but they think if that doesn't work, there's the rubber plant in town, the sneaker factory."

Comedy runs in Leno's veins. At South Elementary School in Andover, Leno used to let the other kids slam his head with a hammer to prove how hard a head he had. Anything for a laugh. Looking back on it, Leno remarked, "Ow! My head would hurt so much."

Young Leno wasn't much of a student. Anyone who would allow people to conk him on the head with a hammer couldn't have had many brain cells to begin with. In fact, doctors pronounced him mildly dyslexic. More like mildly nuts.

One of his guidance counselors was even more critical: She suggested he drop out of school for the good of everyone concerned. Bad news for the class cut-up.

Not all of his teachers were so derogatory. Earl Simon, Leno's fifth-grade teacher, reported, "If James used the effort toward his studies that he uses to be humorous, he'd be an A student. I hope he never loses his talent to make people chuckle."

Leno had his first experience as a comedian in the classroom when a teacher was discussing Robin Hood and his Band of Merry Men.

"You know, people were very cruel back then," the teacher said. "They killed people by boiling them in oil."

Like a pro, Leno saw his opening and took it. "But they couldn't boil Tuck." He paused to build the suspense. Timing is everything in comedy. "He was a friar."

Leno remembers that occasion well. "That was the first time I think I ever told a *joke* joke, a grown-up joke. And I remember thinking, 'Hmmm, that's an interesting reaction.' And since then I've always been able to remember everything I said, good or bad, and the reaction it got. I was never particularly good at remembering names or spelling or adding, but I could always remember what made people laugh."

His mild dyslexia never improved and haunted him throughout his school years. Later on, in his college days, he excelled in classroom lectures, since he remembered everything he heard. What he had trouble with was the reading that went along with the classwork. His mother helped him all she could; it simply took longer for him to translate words on paper into words he could hear.

As a teenager, Leno held several jobs. In high school he worked as a car washer at Wilmington Ford. Cars were in his blood—he also worked at a Boston Ford dealership. Then he worked at McDonald's, which provided grist for his comedy mill when he grew up.

Once, the local McDonald's shops held a talent competition for funniest comedian. Leno decided to enter. He liked being on-stage, and he won a camera for first prize after performing a monologue.

He graduated from Andover High School in 1968. His chosen career, according to the class yearbook, was, in his own words, "re-tired millionaire."

An indifferent student at Bentley College in Waltham at first, then at Emerson College in Boston a year later, Leno sought out the Boston bars to alleviate the boredom of academia. He honed his stand-up comedy routines at saloons.

"I'm a comedian," he would tell the barkeeper.

"Get out of here."

Then Leno would lay down a friendly wager if the bouncer hadn't tossed him out yet. He would plunk down a fifty-dollar bill on the bar and say, "Just let me tell some jokes, and if people leave or I embarrass the customers, you can keep the fifty."

In other words, he had to pay to get people to listen to his jokes at first.

Most of the barkeeps were decent joes. Even when they didn't think he was funny, they returned his fifty dollars. Once in a while they would ask him to return next week for a repeat performance, saying something like, "Hey. You're a funny kid. Why don't you come in next week, and we'll pass the hat?"

Leno could never refuse an invitation like that.

Ironically, while Leno was doing comedy professionally, he was rejected when he tried out for Emerson's comedy workshop. Despite the humiliation of that rejection, he persisted in emceeing campus talent shows, where guitar-strumming teenagers whined about split ends. Enough already, thought Leno. This is sophomoric. It was time to take the next step in his career.

Aching to leave college and get into show biz, he balked at the urge, not wanting to disappoint his parents, who hoped he would finish college in the traditional fashion.

Leno explained, "My parents thought that just to go to college at all was amazing. Their advice was finish college, get your degree, and you can always teach if you can't find something else."

And he had to hold up his end of the sibling competition. His brother, Patrick, was a natural scholar, named one of the top ten students in the country. Jay couldn't drop out after the record his brother had set!

Jay's mother remembered her two very different boys: Patrick very shy; Jay very outgoing. "I was always saying, 'Paddy, go to the school dance, go meet a nice girl.' Seems like I was always pushing Paddy out the door and pulling Jamie, the little devil, back in."

But Leno couldn't work up any excitement for following his parents' educational advice. Instead of graduating from Emerson, he graduated from fifty-buck entry fees at bars to Boston's Combat Zone, the center of the tenderloin district.

Bump-and-grind joints with names like the Kit Kat Club and the Teddy Bear Lounge beckoned him. One cheesy tell-it-like-it-is joint just called itself Nude. Another clip job couldn't even afford to fit all the letters of Leno's name on the ramshackle marquee. Sounding more like a character out of a James Bond novel than a comedian, his name graced the lights as "the talented Mr. No."

Who was this Mr. No? It was "a stupid college kid with long hair and glasses," according to Leno. His amateurish act consisted of stale sociopolitical sixties' humor, such witty lines as "Hey, Nixon. What a jerk! Heh-heh-heh."

Leno can only groan at the memories. This was nothing like his happy childhood.

At one dive he performed in front of two nude strippers who mimed taking sponge baths inside enormous champagne glasses. The two busty, hard-bitten working girls naturally had stage names like Lili Pagan and Ineeda Mann.

As traditionally is their nature, these two strippers had hearts of gold and felt compelled to mother the naive and defenseless Leno.

One night Leno didn't know how to handle a heckler who brought Leno's act to a grinding halt. Ineeda Mann couldn't stand it anymore. She hauled herself out of her giant champagne glass, approached the heckler, socked him in the kisser, broke his nose, and laid him out cold.

Or was it Lili Pagan? Leno can't recall for sure. Whoever it was came back onstage and encouraged Leno after her kayo, piping, "Go ahead, dearie. Do your act." And she did hers, washing her nude body with a sponge.

Petrified, Leno could think of only the one hackneyed joke: "Hey, Nixon. What a jerk!"

Why did Leno get the impression the audience liked the strippers' act better?

Talk about naive. Not only couldn't he handle hecklers, he didn't know how to deal with one of the strippers who, unlike her fellow motherly workers, had a yen for him.

"Hey, kid, how about getting it together later?" she asked him.

Leno was game. And why not? She was curvaceous in the right places. Backstage he looked her up as promised.

"When I came back," he recalls, "there she was, her leg up on a chair, totally naked. There *I* was in my best jacket and nice tie, carrying a box of candy and a bunch of flowers. I was so *naive!*"

Leno has grown to like hecklers over the years, so he says. For his money, they can add to the show if they have any wit at all. "I'm not adversarial onstage. I actually like a good heckler who can keep pace and make the show funnier. But heckling isn't always that cerebral."

What Leno didn't like were certain red-light district bars where patrons, not appreciating his "Nixon, what a jerk!" jokes, flipped burning cigarettes at him onstage and laughed themselves silly as he dodged the flaming projectiles. What made matters worse was that those were the only laughs Leno got.

On nights like those, Leno had to take a long hard look at himself and decide if a career in comedy was a game worth the candle. He decided it was. So what if he had to duck burning cigarettes? His friends were making a puny two dollars an hour waiting tables, whereas he was raking in forty dollars a night with nude bimbos performing onstage with him.

And yet . . . his friends busing tables didn't have to work at dumps like those in Revere Beach on the outskirts of Boston. Cigarette throwing was an art at one particular rattrap. The callow Leno was unprepared even though he should have been tipped off when the owner advised him to wear old clothes for his first appearance at the club.

Leno didn't take the guy's advice. "I want to look nice," Leno told him.

The owner admonished him to be prepared to be pelted with burning coffin nails. Forewarned is forearmed.

Leno would have none of it. He wasn't about to wear rags onstage as he delivered his monologue. If he had looked closer at the owner's outfit he would have noticed a raft of singes on the material.

The owner shrugged. So be it.

During his routine, Leno picked up on bar patrons paying close attention to the lengths of their smoking cigarettes. When the cigarettes burned down to about an inch, the rowdy patrons took a long hit on them, causing them to flare up, and snapped them at Leno, who should have known better than to stand there in his good suit, which, of course, wound up burned in various places, along with his cheeks and hair.

His hair, in fact, emitted such a rank odor as it burned that he gagged on the smell of it. Meanwhile, he winced as the flaming cigarettes stung his cheeks like enraged hornets.

The audience guffawed, laughing *at* Leno, not *with* him.

Said Leno of the incident, "I don't know how this custom originated, but it was like one of those Indian trial-by-fire things. Tough club."

So you want to be a comedian?

Maybe the "Mr. Clean of contemporary comedy"—so called by *Vanity Fair*—couldn't cut it on the hardball strip-joint circuit. Could it be that the barflies wanted blue humor to whet their appetites for another brew?

Leno pointed out, "Everyone just assumes you must be a wimp or a jerk if you're a comic."

However, Leno made no plans to add off-color jokes to his fledgling act. He wasn't going to give up that easily. He would simply try another club.

And he thought Revere Beach was bad. . . .

Wait till he got a load of a hootchie-cootchie club called the Mine Shaft. The name tells it all: The audience got Leno's mine of jokes, and Leno got the shaft.

Picture this: The members of the audience wore phony miners' lamps on their heads as they watched the floor show—*ogled it* is more like it. The show consisted of strippers in their birthday suits strutting around onstage amid the fluttering light beams cast by the coal miners' lamps in the dimly lit bar.

Like a girlie-show huckster, Leno stood off to the side of the stage in the dark and cracked jokes. To his dismay he felt "nobody could see me when I was talking and nobody cared about what I was saying anyway. And when I looked out over the audience, all I could see was a bunch of lights glowing on everybody's heads."

Not an enjoyable experience, but it beat getting turned into a human torch onstage at Revere Beach. Or did it? At least the audience could *see* him at Revere Beach. All they got at the Mine Shaft was a disembodied voice in the darkness.

If this was Leno's future in comedy, he wanted none of it. He had to be able to land gigs at better clubs than at these fleabags. How could he hope to further his career by continuing to work at places with names like the Nameless Coffeehouse and the Sword in the Stone?

He stepped up a rung in the world when he opened one night at a jazz club on the Massachusetts Turnpike. In the "biz" it's known as "a room." The owner, Lennie Sogoloff, used to pay famous jazz musicians to play at his North Shore Jazz Room, more popularly known as Lennie's.

Sogoloff ran an ad in 1972 inviting comedians to try out their acts at his "Monday-night hoots," also known as open-mike shows.

Reading the ad, Leno figured this was just the ticket to boost his stalling career. If he had the moxie to endure the Mine Shaft, surely he could work up the nerve to perform at Lennie's, a more prestigious club by far.

Sogoloff remembered the night. "Jay Leno showed up. He had granny glasses, an Afro, jeans, and the whole sixties look. The audition was like a scene in an old Warner Brothers movie."

When Sogoloff asked him why he was there, Leno said he was a comedian.

"So—make me laugh," Sogoloff dared him.

Half a minute later Sogoloff was in stitches. He named Leno house comic.

Jazz musicians like Mose Allison, Stan Getz, Ahmad Jamal, and Buddy Rich, the renowned drummer who had a habit of showing up on Johnny Carson's *Tonight Show* as the headliner, all frequented Lennie's. On the night Leno opened, Buddy Rich was featured. Yearning to see the kinetic drummer, the crowd booed a woman singing onstage.

"Get off! You're a slut!"

The boisterous crowd reduced her to tears. She choked on her lyrics, her face flushed, and she hightailed it off the stage.

The audience cheered that the nervous wreck had left. "All right! Yeah! Good riddance! Hey! We want Buddy!"

Waiting in the wings, Leno wondered if the singer's wretched fate was what awaited him. He gulped, his blood pressure skyrocketing. Was this place really supposed to be better than the Mine Shaft?

Even the emcee was unnerved. He had never seen a singer so degraded onstage. Was it the end of the poor woman's singing career? Was it the end of her mental stability? In any case, the show must go on.

He put on a phony grin for the pack of animals called an audience in front of him. "We've got a bright young comedian!"

"Comedian this!" yelled the crowd in ungrammatical but clear meaning.

That was pretty tame coming from this bunch of hyenas. He decided to keep going. He introduced the comic Jay Leno.

"We hate him!" somebody hollered.

Great, thought Leno. It didn't intimidate him, though. In fact, it did quite the opposite. It ticked him off.

He strutted onto the stage, his chest puffed out, his head held high, defiant. He wondered how they could possibly hate him—none of them had ever seen him before. They didn't look like a bunch of strip-joint regulars. He had never appeared at a halfway decent club in his life. Why were they giving him the raspberry?

"Thank you very much, great to be here," he said.

The crowd booed him roundly. Catcalls pierced the air, counterpointed by stomping feet.

A bent-nosed wise guy roared, "Hey, get Buddy out here or I'm going to smash your face!"

"Well, sir—" Leno faltered. How was he going to handle this thug? For all he knew, this guy could be a Mafia hit man. If nothing else, he looked the part.

"Get him out here right now or I'm going to bust you up!"

Noting the man's fearsome aspect, Leno decided discretion was the better part of valor. He tried to make friends with the *Godfather* extra by smiling and striking up a genial conversation:

"So, where you from?"

The goon leapt onstage, pounced on Leno, and threw him to the floor. Leno lay there motionless, blood streaming out of his torn scalp.

Sogoloff ambled over to him. "Come on. Get up and finish."

Leno blinked his eyes and took in his surroundings, seeing stars but, unfortunately for him, not the celebrity kind. He tried to focus his gaze on something.

A couple was sitting some ten feet from him, indifferent to his suffering. Maybe they hadn't witnessed the mugging. If they had, they could not have cared less. Not a good sign, figured Leno.

He staggered to his feet with a pounding headache. It was all he could do to avoid falling over. At least he didn't have to worry about the wise guy. At this juncture, two lumberjacklike customers were restraining him with armlocks, preventing him from lunging at Leno again.

Leno took it in stride and, like a good trouper, finished his act.

Sogoloff paid him all of twenty-five dollars. The sum paid, Leno's agent grabbed his ten percent.

"That was the funniest thing," Leno told Tom Shales of *The Washington Post.* "I had to break a five to give him his cut!"

Just a joke. Of course, Leno had no agent at this time. What agent in his right mind would represent a comic starring at a strip club called Nude?

Leno's career couldn't go any further down, so it went up.

He took his act to New York, New York. No stranger to the city, he had visited it several times while working as a part-time mechanic and auto deliveryman for a Boston Mercedes-Benz and Rolls-Royce repair garage.

It was time to do his gig at better-known comedy clubs such as Catch a Rising Star and The Bitter End.

Peter Tauber, a fellow aspiring comedian, met Leno and later, in 1989, described him in the following manner when he wrote an article for *The New York Times Magazine*.

"I am obliged to admit that I have known Jay Leno for years. I first met him in 1973 outside of the original Improvisation nightclub on Forty-fourth Street and Ninth Avenue in New York. He was twenty-three, a bushy-haired kid in wire-rimmed glasses who wanted to be a stand-up comic, as did I for the six months or so I lasted."

Tauber was struck by Leno's "aquamarine eyes" and his resemblance to Elvis Presley. Leno's straight-arrow image had a strong impact on Tauber.

"He didn't smoke, drink, take drugs, tell jokes that demeaned any gender or ethnic group. He was, most other comics agreed, just a nice and funny guy who liked to talk offstage about books he'd read."

As a man who didn't smoke, drink, take drugs, or tell jokes that were off-color or demeaned anyone, Jay Leno was an anomaly in show business. But he adhered to the image. Of course, in some dens in which he worked, he *had* to tell an occasional dirty joke just to keep the audience awake. But generally his average was very much on the clean side.

Since he did not drink, he did not belong to groups who sat around and paid each other off one round at a time. He simply got a reputation as someone who did not buy drinks for anyone.

This was aberrant behavior at the time, yet he managed to keep his image the way he wanted it to be. Even normal teetotalers were astonished that he could get away with what he did, circulating most of his time among show business types. He was as strong-willed as his Scottish mother. He just said no.

As a matter of fact, the reason he didn't tell off-color jokes was that he didn't even *like* them. Yet he did have a handful of them for an emergency. And there were occasions when he was forced to use them to keep on his feet.

Leno recalls some memorable joke attempts at The Bitter End:

"I remember a joke I used to do—terrible joke—about the new male hygiene spray called Umpire, for men with foul balls. That was the joke. Just terrible, awful."

Mostly though, Leno had no real material. Like the scores of other struggling comedians, he had no jokes.

"I used to work Cafe Wha? in the Village," he once said. "Some guy would get up and read a poem: 'Stop your war machine. Thank you.' That would be the poem! Then somebody would say, 'Okay, now we've got a guy who's going to do some comedy for you. Hit it, Jay.' "

And Leno would say, "Hey, Nixon. What a jerk!" No joke. "It wasn't *anything*," he later confessed. "I was just stupid."

If he did have a joke to tell, which was rare, he took so long to tell it that by the time he reached the punch line the audience was nodding off. On balance, his technique was lousy, and he would be the first to admit it.

He once summed up his life in show biz at the time in this fashion: "These were places where people with no money were willing to be entertained by people with no talent."

Undeterred by his joke of a career, he managed to maintain his clean-cut image. "I guess I'm nice. I have no reason not to be. Things have always gone fairly well for me. The real trick in show business is to find something you do well and just do it."

The Wormy Apple

New York wasn't a total bust. Leno contrived to meet Freddie Prinze, David Brenner, and Robert Klein there. Not everyone would end up a comic manqué.

In a sense, it was good for Leno that so few ace comedians were practicing at that time. It meant less competition for him.

On a gig at Catch a Rising Star, only two comedians showed up for an audition. Beside Leno, the other one happened to be Freddie Prinze. That made it a piece of cake for both of them to get hired.

It therefore comes as no surprise that Leno loved New York, where "getting on was easy."

Even so, it took years for him to achieve any kind of recognition and success there. His early experiences remained indelibly engraved in his mind. He can even recall the first joke he told at The Bitter End in the early seventies:

"You could do anything in your room at college. You could smoke pot, live in a coed dorm, have a girl. But you couldn't have . . . a hot plate!" Leno mimicked a bumptious college dean on the phone. "Mrs. Leno? This is the dean. We've got your son Jay—yes, it was on suspicion of soup. The lab boys say it was *definitely* Campbell's cream of mushroom."

Sure, it was a lame joke, but Leno later excused himself. "Hey! I was only in the business a *week.*"

To support himself he continued making deliveries for the Boston auto dealership where he worked. He drove to New York twenty-four times before landing a gig at the original Improvisation, where the other would-be comedians watched him in awe as he pulled up to the club in a different Rolls-Royce for each of his nighttime appearances.

Leno's comedy career was proving a long row to hoe, but he enjoyed his profession and had no desire to leave it—even if it was paying peanuts.

He may not have been coining money but he was getting noticed by the critics. A *Variety* critic wrote a rave review for his impression of Elvis impersonating Hamlet singing the famous prince of Denmark's soliloquy.

Leno loved the life of Riley the comedic profession affords to its practitioners. Where else could he stand up in front of an audience, chat nonstop, and get paid for the effort? For Leno's money, no other professional has it this easy.

Not all critics lauded Leno's act. A Boston promoter, Fred Taylor, saw Leno's routine in 1972 and said:

"I wouldn't have given Leno a whole lot of odds on becoming

a star. Material-wise, he was sharp. He was current-event savvy. The newspaper was his resource. He was intellectually astute, yet funny, but he needed timing. He needed the body movements onstage. He needed to move from spoken-word funny to theatrical funny. I give him a whole lot of credit. For him, becoming a star was strictly a bootstrap operation."

Leno's own relatives didn't think much of his routine. Leno told Dick Lochte, a writer for *Playboy,* that he once invited his relatives to watch him at The Bitter End.

Leno did the show on Tuesday for no pay, as that was the custom at The Bitter End. Ebullient, Leno informed his relatives and, equally happy, they decided to attend the show to offer moral support.

His basically square relatives didn't know what they were in for. They didn't expect the chichi joint with its posthippie ambience or pot smoke and patchouli incense. The all-but-empty watering hole catered to the au courant set, not to the conservative middle-class Lenos.

Leno got a kick out of watching his kin enter the place. He remembers well "Uncle Lou with the big hat," his ninetyish grandma "with the aluminum walker," and various and sundry other uncles and aunts parading to their seats. And how could he forget his grandma clapping and yelping out with delight, "Jamie onna da stage. Jamie onna da stage"?

It was a heart-warming moment for Leno. As he mounted the stage he became self-conscious and tongue-tied. Here he was in front of his family and all he had in his script were "sophomoric dirty jokes."

He hung fire, suffering stage fright, an unusual experience for him. No way was he going to deliver his cut-and-dried collection of dirty jokes. There was nothing else for it but to clean up his act. Sanitizing his monologue, he reeled off cliché after cliché of G-rated humor. He couldn't wait to get off the stage, even as the audience offered their plaudits for his work.

All of the audience save the Leno family, that is. Leno discovered that they had left "maybe seven minutes after getting there, emptying the place for the next act."

So much for the concept that blood is thicker than water.

Leno learned there, as well as elsewhere, that audiences enjoyed his white-bread jokes. They liked his nice-guy image. He could do the ethnic, racist, and sexist jokes as well as the next guy, but they didn't jibe with his image and therefore they didn't sell when he relied on them.

Describing his current reliance on squeaky-clean material, he said, "It's a marketing decision, not a moral one. I find I get more laughs working clean."

He goes out of his way to make sure he doesn't offend anyone, hewing to the politically correct line. Later in his career, when he was performing on Johnny Carson's show he had, for him, a nerve-racking moment, which he recalls thus:

"I did a joke one night when the movie *The Last Temptation of Christ* came out. I said a group of fundamentalists wanted to buy the movie back from the producers for ten million dollars to destroy it because they felt it was morally offensive. And that Warner Brothers was trying to contact the same group to see if they wanted *Caddyshack II*."

It mortified Leno when he received a two-page typewritten letter chewing him out for his "five-minute attack on our Lord Jesus Christ." The letter writer went on, "I used to like you, and I had tickets to see you, but I tore them up and threw them away." And more to the same effect.

As is his wont whenever he receives critical mail, he called up the letter writer to find out what had cheesed her off.

The woman who wrote the letter told him she had not seen the show she had lambasted. A friend of hers had seen it and described to her how Leno had insulted Jesus Christ.

"The problem is that people don't listen," observed Leno. "When I'm on Carson, it's eleven-thirty at night, people are half-asleep, and there are certain things you just can't say because they won't hear you correctly."

Between jobs in New York City, Leno flew out to Los Angeles to work a couple of clubs. His budding career fizzled and he returned to New York, where, wormy though the Big Apple was, acceptance came easier. He may not have been a household word yet, but he was making his mark in the Manhattan clubs.

Leno still made his residence in Andover despite working the clubs predominantly in New York. His comedian buddies such as Richard Lewis, Freddie Prinze, Jimmie Walker, and Billy Crystal frequented his Andover apartment, which became a well-known hangout for comedians. Barbara Isaacs of the *Rochester* (New York) *Democrat and Chronicle* called it a "fabled spot," a kind of shrine for funnymen, thanks to the droves of them who put up there at one time or another.

None other than Freddie Prinze bunked there more than once. On one stay he brought a gun with him—not surprising, since he eventually died from a self-inflicted gunshot wound to the head.

He lugged the gun to Leno's digs and commenced horsing around with it, terrifying Leno and his pals by discharging rounds inside the apartment.

Leno claims Prinze went through no less than three hundred cartridges of ammo in the living room, blowing a hole in the wall so huge you could see through it.

Leno felt lucky to escape with his life. He has no idea what got into Prinze on that visit. The incident left Leno on edge for days. What in the world would he tell the landlord?

Richard Lewis was there with Prinze and asserts that the bullet holes in the walls didn't change the appearance of the apartment all that much. The place could hardly be called neat to begin with. A half-inch layer of snack foods carpeted the floor, causing a corn chip to become forever embedded in Lewis's spine after he lay back on the floor once.

Leno had his own joke for response. "That's just classic persnickety Lewis. Lewis washes his hands forty times a day. The apartment could *never* be clean enough for him."

During his early career, Leno ventured to the Cellar Door in Washington, D.C. It reminded him of Boston's red-light hootchie-cootchie district.

When he walked onstage and said, "Hi, everybody," it was as if he had ignited a bomb. All hell broke loose. Then, before he was aware of it, a patron sneaked up behind him and cold-cocked him with a ketchup bottle—*full* of ketchup no less. Welcome to the nation's capital, Jay.

The blow decked him. He lay there, out cold on the stage. The audience laughed its head off at him. They couldn't get enough of it. They thought it was Leno's impersonation of a guy getting mugged on Pennsylvania Avenue.

It made him long for the days of Ineeda Mann's strip dive.

Then there was the time he journeyed to the City of Brotherly Love. In Philly he performed at the Main Point, patronized by many blacks who dug the jazz riffs there. Leno met the blind man Rahsaan Roland Kirk, a talented artist who was way ahead of his time and could play tunes through his nose. He even spouted "black nationalist rap" with the fervor of a prophet.

Leno chatted with Kirk backstage and asked him to introduce him at the end of Kirk's act. Nothing loath, Kirk agreed. As Kirk delivered a scathing attack on the white establishment that was bent on subverting the brothers, Leno perused the audience, which consisted mainly of blacks wearing shades.

Listening to Kirk, they began muttering, "Right on!" and "Get whitey!"

Interesting crowd, thought Leno.

Then he heard Kirk intone, "I'd like to introduce you to a *brother* who's going to entertain you!" He waited a beat. "And here he is! *Brother* Jay Leno!"

Leno sidled onto the stage in front of the surly faces glowering at him, worried after he had heard Kirk say *brother*. At the sight of him, there was a stone-dead silence in the crowd. Followed by sotto voce curses and snarls directed at him.

Breaking into a cold sweat, Leno eyeballed the sea of black faces before him and gesticulated amiably at Kirk. "Hey. Maybe you haven't *noticed*." A pause of two beats. "Rahsaan's . . . blind!"

Stating the obvious broke the audience up. They rolled in the aisles and were putty in Leno's hands for the rest of the night.

*   *   *

As terrifying as his first ordeal in Washington, D.C., had been, he returned there in 1973 to appear with Rare Earth at George Washington University. Rare Earth was a hit singing group at the time.

"I came down to the university," said Leno, "and the audience is all neighborhood kids from the area—mostly teenagers, mostly boys about fifteen years old."

Rare Earth's manager buttonholed Leno as Leno entered the gymnasium, which had been transformed into a jerry-built auditorium for the sake of the concert.

The manager scowled at Leno. "Hey, listen. Rare Earth's got a lot of expensive equipment on the stage. You can't use the stage. You've got to stand on the gym floor."

No big deal, thought Leno. He agreed, expecting no problems.

Standing on the floor delivering his monologue, he was surrounded by an audience that left little room for him to maneuver in. If he had been claustrophobic he would have fainted on the spot. Maybe this was what they meant by the term *in your face*.

"Anybody here from Boston?" Leno prattled into his mike, whose cord meandered along the floor into the crowd.

Somebody apparently didn't cotton to Boston. At that moment the mike jerked out of Leno's hand and shot into the gaggle of teenagers ensconcing him. As the mike skipped across the varnished floorboards, a resonant booming deafened everyone.

Egg on his face, Leno darted after the errant mike amid uproarious laughter. Trying to shag it, he heard a guy rib him with the words, "Hey, bro—what's happening?"

"Give me that!" Leno screamed. "Give me that mike!"

At length he tracked down the cord and, following it, he came upon the end, which dangled in his hand minus the mike. It turned out to be one of the shortest monologues Leno ever delivered.

When he tried to get the manager to pay him, the manager protested, "The mike is your responsibility."

Was this guy for real?

"They docked me seventy-five dollars out of my pay for it," said Leno. "It was all so stupid. It was the most *horrible* job. I mean, unbelievable. But that's show biz!"

After his debacle with the mike, Leno could commiserate with Rodney Dangerfield's pet beef about getting no respect.

Then there was the time at the notorious Study Hall C in up-state New York. A sorority paid Leno twenty-five bucks a night to do a three-night stand at Study Hall C.

"So I go to Study Hall C," recalled Leno. "There's a thumbtack with an index card on the door: 'Tonight: Jay Leno.' Doesn't say what I do or anything."

Inside Study Hall C, to the surprise of no one, the students were studying and paid no attention to his entrance. The six sorority girls who had invited him showed up and announced, "Okay, everybody! We have a comedy show here!"

A student grimaced. "Hey, shut up! We have a test!"

The sorority girls couldn't have cared less. They were bound and determined to put on their show. One of them gave Leno a mike for one hand and a speaker for the other. Not great acoustics but what could you expect at a study hall?

Leno trained the speaker at whoever bothered to look at him as he told his jokes. For forty-five minutes he plowed ahead like a good soldier before a crowd of uninterested and downright rude students.

Several of them covered their ears with their hands and shrieked, "Why don't you just get out of here and go home? You're not funny. You're—*stupid*!"

After one night at Study Hall C, Leno was bushed. He couldn't face another night of student apathy and hostility.

"Listen, girls," he told the members of the sorority that had hired him, "this isn't going to work out."

"Oh?" one of them said snottily. "Well, we're going to call your agent and tell him you're *uncooperative*!"

Do and be damned, Leno felt like saying, but, nice guy that he was, he decided to come back and perform the following night.

It was déjà vu. Like a recurring nightmare. On the second night he entered the study room and the same ill-bred brats were there waiting to let him have it.

"We saw you last night!" a student called out. "Shut up, you're not funny. Why don't you go home?"

On the third night it was open season on Leno for the sorority girls who hired him. That night as he was eating in the cafeteria before the show, a clutch of them walked by him. One turned up her nose at the sight of him and whispered to her friends, "There's that jerk that thinks he's a comedian."

Another humiliating incident occurred in Buffalo, New York, when Leno tried to audition for a gig on television in the early seventies. The degradation was so foul he could taste it.

The show was called *A.M. Buffalo*. Leno stood in the green room with a group of performers who claimed to be authentic pygmy dancers. At least they looked the part—what with the bones in their noses, their grass skirts, and the long spears they sported.

They couldn't speak English, grunted to each other as a form of communication, and ignored Leno.

When the talent coordinator walked into the green room he had the gall to ask Leno and the spear-carrying pygmies the following: "Mr. *Lenooooo*?"

The coordinator was looking at all of them and for the life of him couldn't single out Leno. The coordinator kept cutting his eyes around the room waiting for a response or some kind of revelation.

Leno decided he had better clue the guy in, but the coordinator rubbed salt in the wound by adding, "Which one is Mr. Leno?"

It was enough to make Leno take a powder.

New Jersey wasn't much better. There a man hired him to pretend he was Bob Carlyle, director of sales for an unspecified company. Impersonating Bob Carlyle, Leno was supposed to perform his monologue and crack up the audience.

The seventy-five or so mid-level executives who sat in the audience actually liked Leno. They didn't go hog wild in their appreciation but he did hear a few claps in the audience. Maybe they figured he was funny—for a director of sales.

As the applause died down, the guy who hired Leno mounted the stage and exclaimed, "Okay! That, of course, was *not* my director of sales, but Jay Leno—a professional comedian!"

With that he told them the real reason he had assembled them. He wanted to give them gratis a special dispenser kit. The members of the audience were bona fide drugstore representatives. The kit they were presented with was a new product called Fresh'n.

"This product will revolutionize personal hygiene!" declared Leno's employer.

"What is it?" shouted a rep.

Leno winced when he heard the response. The product was a damp towelette used to eradicate "embarrassing rectal odor," as his employer put it.

A chorus of groans.

The hall emptied so fast the man barely had time to tell everyone: "Wait! I've got two hundred thousand of these in my warehouse. I want you to have one free—to take them. Please!" he begged them. "Take a dozen! Put them in your stores! No charge! Please!"

Leno couldn't get out of there fast enough either. Being nice was one thing, but being so polite as to take a Fresh'n was something else again.

Leno is the kind of guy whose niceness prompts him to help little old ladies across the street. One time, out of character, he barged onto an airplane, elbowing his way past an old woman in a wheelchair.

She was the picture of tact as she waved for him to go on ahead. "Oh, go ahead, dearie."

Leno couldn't stand himself after that. "I felt like the guy on the *Titanic* who puts on a dress so he can get in the life raft first."

He vowed never again to behave rudely or to act superior like a cad. It wasn't in his nature to do it. Even when he became a celebrity he continued to eschew the lifestyle of a prima donna.

As he put it, "I don't need ten guys feverishly sorting through bags of M&Ms because I don't like green ones. I just want a glass of water and a stool."

Another adventure for Leno in the subterranean ghetto of the comedy profession took place in the Midwest. It wasn't only the East Coast that had seedy clubs.

"There was a midway in Minnesota where I stood doing my

gig between the pig-elephant tent and the half-woman/half-snake exhibit. The half-woman/half-snake had a picture of Liz Taylor pasted over a snake. But *inside* the tent, there was a horrible fetus with a snake attached to it. You had to pay a quarter to see it."

Leno would rather pay a quarter *not* to see it. It was uglier than that monster in *Alien*.

In the end, it made no difference what jokes he told at the Minnesota gig, since nobody could hear his voice, lost amid the cacophony of the screeching steam calliope and the squealing children riding the Ferris wheel.

Leno was a bear for punishment in the early days of his career. No matter how bad the gigs got, he kept returning for more—and it paid off. He landed more TV exposure, which couldn't help but serve as a boon to his aspirations in the field of comedy.

Not that all of his TV auditions were successful. . . .

When he tried out for the *Jack Paar Tonight* show in the early seventies, he was standing outside the talent coordinator's office with a bevy of would-be show-biz performers when the talent coordinator ambled by him and singled him out for a piece of contemptuous advice, starting with the question, "Is *that* the suit you're going to wear on the show?"

Feeling self-conscious for being singled out from the other auditioners by the sneering talent coordinator, Leno managed to squeak, "Yeah."

"Listen. Go on home. This isn't for you."

As if his gigs weren't bad enough, the accommodations he put up with when performing were even worse.

The most disgusting fleabag he lodged at, bar none, was the

one in Cincinnati. This baby wasn't fit for a Skid Row bum. At three dollars a night it was highway robbery. As unbelievable as it sounds, it had a toilet in the center of it. In the late watches of the night, a sound woke him from his slumbers. He couldn't identify it, but he determined that it was emanating from the hallway beyond his door. In the sliver of the corridor's light shining beneath the door, he spotted water flowing into his room.

Puzzled, he decided to investigate.

He approached the door and opened it, careful not to step in the puddle.

In the hallway a geezer was taking a leak against Leno's door without a care in the world.

"What are you doing?" asked Leno, pissed off, so to speak.

The geezer pulled a face. "Oh! I'm sorry. I *always* urinate on this door."

Leno studied the door. He had to hand it to the old guy. The whole lower corner of the door was rotten. He was telling the truth. It was his door.

In the late sixties, Leno, struggling to improve his act, gave a whirl at working with a partner onstage. His partner, Gene Braunstein, later became a story editor on the TV sitcom *Who's the Boss?* The inauspicious pairing ended almost as soon as it began.

Then Leno joined an improv group called Fresh Fruit Cocktail. In fact, he beat out Braunstein in the competition for the job. Fresh Fruit Cocktail worked the Playboy Club as well as other clubs several cuts above the comedy hell of Study Room C.

For his part, Leno hated every minute of it. He found he didn't like working with other people because it made him too dependent on them. "I never liked team sports as a kid. I never understood the concept."

Needless to say, his association with Fresh Fruit Cocktail didn't last long.

A turning point in his career came in 1974 when he was plumped down in front of his TV set in his Andover apartment watching *The Tonight Show Starring Johnny Carson.*

In an epiphany of insight, he realized as he sat there that the stand-up comic performing on the show was lousy. If this tragedy could get booked on the Carson show, why couldn't Leno? For sure, his act couldn't be any worse than this pathetic so-called attempt at the comic arts.

He set his legendary jaw in determination. He would move to Hollywood and take a flier at establishing his comedy career there.

The way Leno saw it was, "If I stay here in Boston, I'm going to acquire all the things that make life comfortable. Then I'll never get a real shot at the top of the comedy pyramid."

He believed there was a hierarchy in comedy, as in every business, and Hollywood had the top bananas.

Leaving his apartment, he told his neighbors, "Good-bye. I'm going to Hollywood. You want anything, take it."

He traveled light as he caught the next red-eye to LAX. So what if he didn't have much money. He would make it big time in the show-biz capital of the world.

Had he failed, he could always find a job in another area of the comedy life. So went his thinking, in any case.

But as everybody knows now, he didn't fail—far from it.

The Left Coast

The year was 1974, and, his wallet thin, Leno chose to stay overnight at other comics' digs rather than pony up for an apartment of his own which—this being Los Angeles—cost an arm and a leg. A couple of times he even slept in the 1955 Buick Roadmaster he had bought on arrival. Naturally one of the first things he did was buy a car, since he wouldn't be caught dead without one, especially in a city like Los Angeles, whose widespread areas and remote locales were for all practical purposes *created* to be serviced by Detroit's dream boats.

The Big Orange was hard on Leno at first. It could be an unforgiving city for show-biz aspirants.

Twenty-four at the time, virtually unknown, penniless, Leno would "meet a kindly waitress who would let you use the toilet, and then you'd drive across town to use someone else's shower." Leno once noted, "It's handy training—if you ever have to hide out from the police."

Leno can remember the experience as if it were yesterday. "When I landed in L.A., I hitched a ride out to the Sunset Strip. Then I walked and walked to the Comedy Store and hung out there until it opened. I went on that night, and luckily they liked me."

The truth be known, he had to work there for free, but it was so much fun it didn't feel like work. "I like to look upon those first few months as my 'romantic' period."

It wasn't long before he became a regular at the Comedy Store and the Improv.

As long as he was onstage cracking jokes, he was happy. It didn't matter in those days that he was just barely eking out a precarious living with his comedy routines.

Doing stand-up was always "the most soothing, calming part of the day," he pointed out. "I mean, you're onstage, you have no problems, nothing. You're seeing smiling faces, people at their best. Most people don't see [that many] people in a day, let alone . . . people who are smiling and laughing all the time. I'm always more rested after a show than before it."

The important thing for him was that, despite earning mere pin money, he kept working at his trade. He always felt it was necessary for a comedian to practice his art. In other words, as the saying went, use it or lose it.

"The idea is not to fall into the Peter Principle—in the sense that, if you're used to working every night, you're sharper than if you play once a week. A lot of comics figure, Well, I'll just do one night instead of working the week. Then they think they're doing so well they cut back to working just twice a month. Then once every two months. Pretty soon, you don't have any act left."

Leno never took his act to bed with him. That was a bit too much. "I don't crawl into bed wearing a plaid jacket or anything like that. I try to keep in a reasonable frame of mind at home. Actually, my life is pretty normal, pretty much like everybody else's, I suppose."

Being in public always struck him as a part of his lifestyle. "I know when I was a kid and was watching for my favorite comedian on a show, and he'd just come on and sit there and talk and not be funny, I'd be disappointed. And so I always want to be funny. I don't want to go on a game show or judge something."

The thing was, whether early or late in his career—comedy, to him, was always the same. "You get out there and tell jokes. If they laugh, you get paid. If they don't laugh, you don't get paid." Or if you do get paid, nobody'll attend your next performance.

"It's about as basic a business as you can get. With the exception of the microphone, the level of technology is zero. It hasn't changed, really, since the Council of Trent. One guy gets up and talks, the other people listen. It's as ancient, low-tech, and primitive as there is. Except for the occasional snaillike pace of the language, there's really no progress."

Eventually he got his break, more or less. He appeared on several television talk shows—among them Merv Griffin's, Mike Douglas's, and David Letterman's.

One night at the Comedy Store in 1975, the man himself, Johnny Carson, at the behest of Harvey Korman, visited the club and watched Leno. It turned out to be an unpropitious moment for Leno. Carson sat through the show, shaking his head.

As Leno put it, "Johnny said that, Yeah, it was funny, but there weren't enough jokes."

Leno found out about Carson's criticism and, peeved, sneaked into the parking lot with a full supply of eggs and let Carson's blue-chip car have it.

Later, after he had cooled down a bit, Leno mulled over the great man's words and decided that the king of late-night talk was right. "I realized then that the trick is to get as many jokes into the shortest space possible. Take that hour and a half of material you have and make it the funniest five minutes in the world."

To learn from the master, Leno studied Carson's show every night. "I went home and watched *The Tonight Show* religiously and realized that Johnny Carson was doing about fifteen to twenty jokes in the time I took to do four or five. He was right. I still feel badly that I egged his car . . . but not much."

Three years after his arrival in L.A., on March 2, 1977, Leno got the break he had been biding his time for. It was his dream gig—an appearance on Carson's *Tonight Show.*

Over the years a host of comedians had been tooting Leno's horn to Carson—guys like Steve Martin, who was instrumental in getting Leno on the show. Martin talked his contacts at *The Tonight Show* into allowing Leno to perform on the prestigious program. These contacts had Carson's ear and persuaded the king to acquiesce.

Leno could never thank Martin enough. "I'm very grateful to Steve Martin. I appeared on *The Tonight Show* thanks to him, and he didn't know me from a hole in the wall."

Remembering Martin's help, Leno decided he would aid any and all wannabe comedians who needed a boost to their unformed careers. He proceeded to advance Dennis Miller's career after catching his act on *Saturday Night Live*. Even got him an apartment to live in in L.A.

"You take care of one another in this business," Leno pointed out.

Leno's career did not skyrocket after his appearance on *The Tonight Show*. His phone did not ring off the hook.

In short, he was not an overnight success. National exposure on Carson's show did not make him an instant household name. Like fine wine, he had to age some more before peaking.

"When I did my first *Tonight Show*, I did fine, sat down, the phone didn't ring, nothing particularly happened. I was always somebody who had to do a hundred shows instead of ten, and then people would say, 'Oh, there's some funny stuff.' "

For Leno, it was an unforgettable moment. "Your first *Tonight Show* is kind of like your first girl, you know. I mean, it's real fast. It's over real quick. You weren't very good. You never forget it. But you do know you want to do it again. And do it better the next time."

As his career did not take off into orbit on that one appearance on the Carson show, Leno had to continue to work the national club circuit to keep his career going. In fact, Carson did invite Leno back seven or eight times after his initial endeavor, but the stints did nothing to stimulate Leno's image on the tube. Incredibly, his routines began deteriorating to such a degree that after those first gigs he wasn't asked back on *Tonight* for eight—count 'em—*eight* years!

He was twenty-seven years old when he debuted on the Carson show. His income was soaring, in spite of what he thought of as his career on stall. He was making money hand over fist because he was a workaholic. He flew anywhere in the country to do a gig—anywhere they'd have him. And he got the gigs. Sometimes he did two a day. He thrived on travel, loved to get out among people. And the money rolled in.

He had always been able to make out, even when he was in high school and when he first started to work the Boston area. It wasn't the money that bothered him now; that wasn't what he was after. He knew instinctively that his future was on the cathode ray tube—the television set. And to have television's icon, Carson, whisk him aside as if he wasn't worth a puff of dust annoyed him. It made him more determined than ever to get on that tube and show the whole country just how good he was.

And so as the seventies whipped by and the eighties appeared on the horizon, Leno became a money-making machine and traveled to every distant hamlet he could find that would have him. He loved the people he entertained. He loved to tell jokes. He tightened up his style and his routines somewhat, and got better in front of people.

But at no time did he forget that his main target was television. That was what he was after.

One day in the early nineteen eighties as Leno walked along the streets of New York on his way to a gig in Manhattan, a homeless person sidled up to him, holding out a tin cup and crying, "Change! Change!" There weren't as many homeless walking the streets then as now, but there were enough.

Leno smiled at the panhandler. "All I got is paper money, and you want change." He reached out and stuffed a bill into the man's tin cup. As he turned away, he gave him a word of advice: "You got to shoot higher!"

Money. Short and sweet. That was the name of the game. Ben

Franklin knew what money was all about: "Nothing but money is sweeter than honey."

Leno's take on the same subject was only slightly different: "I'm convinced that certain facts of life are disguised by the powers that be to keep poor people from seeing how much fun it is to be rich. I mean, I've been broke and I've had money, and it's a lot of *fun* having money."

Even in his early days, Leno never had any complaints about his professional money-making capabilities as a comic. "I've always been quite happy with my rate of success. Even when I was twenty-six, twenty-seven years old, I was making about twenty thousand dollars a year, which, in those days, was fine. It was a lot of work, but that's all right. It gave me the opportunity to learn, to be bad without anybody knowing about it."

At the outset of his career he had felt like a whore, but he wasn't afraid to absorb his knocks. It was all part of the game. "I say that half kiddingly. Being a comic is sort of like being a prostitute. When you start out, it's humiliating and degrading. But [in time] you get a hundred dollars in a half hour. And when you make money like that, you can't go back to doing something for three or four bucks an hour."

Leno's hardscrabble life didn't last long, and anyway he was having fun cracking jokes, even if he wasn't making oodles of cash. "It's fun. But what's so unbelievable is that they are actually paying me money to have this much fun."

It didn't take Leno long to start making good money as a traveling comic. One Saturday he garnered $25,000 performing at a university in the daytime and another $30,000 at another college that same night. At an average of three hundred gigs a year, he could make a very comfortable living indeed. But that was small beer compared to the millions he would earn one day as host of *The Tonight Show.*

What did he do with the truckloads of money he earned? He bought cars. Also, he said later, "I take care of my folks, my wife's family. I bought my father a car, my brother a car."

Leno's father once said, "Jay's only regret is that we already have a house. He would like to buy us one."

Leno's philosophy at the inception of his career was to do cheap gigs for the valuable experience they provided, with the hope that later the experience would pay off. In his case, it did—in spades. Eventually.

He even earned a chance to appear at Las Vegas. It was an experience he would rather forget. He played second fiddle to singer Tom Jones. Leno's job was to be the opening act for Jones.

What riled him was the cold shoulder he got at the ticket booth when he tried to purchase tickets to his own show for a friend. The cashier told Leno Tom Jones didn't have an opening act.

"No. *I'm* the opening act," huffed Leno.

"Uh, sir, I don't think so," said the cashier.

That did it. Leno had had his fill of Vegas. "I didn't want to come back until I could at least headline," he said. "I don't mean that in a snobby way. But I'd rather go to little teeny-weeny places where people come to see *me.*"

Why should he have to suffer having his ego bashed by a two-bit cashier in a ticket booth? Thanks, but no thanks.

Years later he would return to Vegas triumphant, his name headlining the marquee.

As long as he kept working, he was happy. He never could understand why everyone else preferred vacationing to working.

"This must be the first time in American history when it's considered strange to work hard! I don't want to sit on a beach! This is what I do! But people think there must be something psychologically wrong with me."

As he became more successful in Los Angeles, he observed the difference between Hollywood and his hometown of Andover once in an interview he had in *Rolling Stone*. "In Los Angeles, they want to know where you were *positioned* in the magazine. In Andover, it's 'Wow! *Rolling Stone.*' They're impressed if you even have a *subscription* to it."

Ever the happy camper, Leno wonders why people kept asking him what he wanted to be doing five years hence. "I don't understand why no one wants to be doing what they're doing. Actors want to sing, singers want to act. But people are annoyed when I say that. Like, somehow, I should want to take up modern dance."

Even when he had become a Hollywood celebrity, Leno never went Hollywood like other celebrities, such as Eddie Murphy, who traveled with a large retinue of bodyguards and the like whenever he went to airports and hotels. Leno hauled his own luggage. "I don't like having handmaidens."

Though rich, Leno wouldn't patronize luxury restaurants. He usually chose an eating place for its view of the parking lot. He wanted to watch his car in the lot, making certain that the valet, or anyone else for that matter, didn't monkey around with one of his precious cars. Food played second banana to automobiles for Leno. After all, this was L.A., car capital of America. Leno wouldn't be caught dead at Spago or Morton's. They don't cater to the ordinary type of blue-collar guy he represented.

"I'm more likely to be seen at Tail o' the Pup or Hard Times Pizza. Maybe Marino down on Melrose. Or Santo Pietro in Beverly

Glen. I'm not real fancy. I'm on the road so much that when I get home, eating out isn't all that important.

"I've finally gotten to the point where I tell people I'd rather just meet them *after* dinner. I guess I've reached that level of success where I don't *have* to go to dinner anymore.

"Anyway, I really come from the stand-over-the-sink world of eating."

Leno could never for the life of him understand people who shelled out a wad of money for dinner. "People will tell me they spent a hundred and twenty dollars on a meal in a restaurant, and *I'll* be genuinely shocked."

For him, "I still enjoy watching extravagant lifestyles more than being a part of them. When I was living in New York trying to be a comedian, I'd go to the Stage Deli, where a roast-beef sandwich cost four dollars and fifty cents. I couldn't bring myself to spend four-fifty on a sandwich, so I'd get a hamburger for a dollar ten."

Leno was a skinflint when it came to food. On the other hand, when it came to cars, he'd pony up vast sums to acquire one he desired.

Why did certain writers pick on him for his teeming wealth? Leno wondered. So what if he was loaded? Was it a crime to be a moneybags?

"I don't really lead a particularly exciting life," he countered. "I have never, ever said in an interview what I make *or* how much I got for a particular job. I don't call myself a millionaire comic. It's very embarrassing. I work exactly as hard if not harder than I ever did when I wasn't making any money."

Leno fell back on the working-man's ethic he had been brought up with. "If I'm gonna work, I might as well work every night." He turned thoughtful. "It's like sitting on a pot of boiling water.

All you've got to do is keep the lid on. My career is sort of like watching the hands of a clock. They don't appear to move until you come back a year or two later and you go, 'Oh, look!' People forget I've been doing this for a long time already."

Struggling with his television career, Leno also tried vainly to get used to the fast-lane lifestyle of L.A.

According to Leno, "If God doesn't destroy Sunset Strip, He owes an apology to Sodom and Gomorrah."

He also said, "In Los Angeles, you have all those dramatic types who introduce themselves, 'Hi, I'm Susan, and this is my *lover*, Bob.' My lover? Shut up! Why don't you just lie down and do it for us right now?"

Jeez, what a town! "I know people who finish their act and say, 'I've got to get drunk and have some sex in this town.' When I finish my act, I go back to my room and watch television, or I'll go out for pizza with a friend. I'm hopelessly American. If something doesn't come in a Styrofoam box with a lid on it, I'm lost."

Not that he ever regretted his settling down in California. "I wasn't married. I had no family to raise. There was no reason to."

Careerwise, they were eight long, unproductive years for Leno to weather—those between his first stint of appearances on *The Tonight Show* and his return. Yet he continued to work his fingers to the bone. His future wife, Mavis, described his hardworking life for these years: "Jay went through a long desert space between being good enough to open shows for other performers and being good enough to open for himself."

His career did not really hit the skids, or anything like that. Comedy clubs throughout the nation were still eager to book him.

The problem was that as far as *The Tonight Show* was concerned, his career was *finis*.

"I remember how all through my career, every four or five years I would be dropped by one or another of the major talent agencies, always for the same reason: I was not the kind of guy who could get his name in the newspapers on a regular basis. An agent once said that to me in just those words. I remember thinking at the time, You know, you're right. I'm not the kind of guy who can get his name into the paper on a regular basis. It's not what I do. I'm not outrageous. I don't drink or smoke or run around."

Acting like "Robo-comic," as Jerry Seinfeld nicknamed him, Leno would make over 250 appearances a year across the country. He would fly anywhere to do a gig, even to a remote club on a North Carolina island where customers had to be rowed in. He felt "he had to go to where the people are."

The TV networks couldn't have cared less how many clubs he played in a year. They kept their distance from him. They considered him untelegenic with his Frankenstein demeanor, yet not loony enough to be really *funny*-ha-ha.

During his eight-year hiatus from television, Leno met a man who would come to mean a great deal to him and who, as a close friend and as a competitor, would later be associated with him in a dramatic and unforgettable fashion.

The man's name was David Letterman. The place where they met was the Comedy Store. The year was 1975, and after they met, Letterman almost immediately became one of Leno's most ardent supporters.

Leno first spotted Letterman when Letterman did a bit on the

Comedy Store stage. Leno was watching the auditions from the back of the auditorium, a practice he had adopted to study the work of his fellow comedians. Always on the lookout for funny material and offbeat presentations, he enjoyed watching new comics. He found it a learning experience. Maybe he could add some of their comedic acumen to his own repertoire to improve it.

The talent that day was not really up to snuff—until Letterman took the stage. Leno had seen him earlier pulling into the Comedy Store parking lot in a pickup truck. Sporting a beard, Letterman brought Dinty Moore to mind as he stepped out of his pickup. It would be easy to mistake Letterman's picture for Moore's on a can of beef stew, Leno figured. What kind of an act could this Indiana bumpkin have?

Leno had all but decided to call it a night, discouraged by the lack of talent onstage, when Letterman trod the boards. Mesmerized by the lilting, persuasive voice, Leno decided to stay a bit. Letterman would tell jokes like, "We are diametrically opposed to the use of orphans as yardage markers on driving ranges"—jokes that would crack Leno up.

Cool and controlled, Letterman had a sophisticated delivery—in spite of his appearance—that impressed Leno as being light years ahead of all his contemporaries.

At the conclusion of Letterman's act, Leno ran up and shook hands with him, saying, "Gee! You've got great stuff."

The respect was mutual. Letterman had already seen Leno and later claimed that Leno had a "huge influence" on his career. "After I saw Jay work for the first time in nineteen seventy-five, I said, 'Oh, *that's* the way it's supposed to be done.' What I was seeing then was Jay Leno on a very bad night."

Leno on Letterman: "He was head and shoulders above anybody else. I patterned much of what I did on what I saw him do. It's no surprise to any of us that he's gotten so successful. I think everybody was surprised that it took him a little longer. The first night I saw him, I thought the next day he was going to be a huge star."

Leno continued to plug away, gamely attempting to carve a niche for himself in the comedy profession—with little effect. An overnight success in Hollywood like Robin Williams or Billy Crystal he was not.

Leno's wife, Mavis, explained the reasons why. "The main way to do that is by getting a starring role in a TV show. But Jay was not considered good-looking, and his comedy isn't wacky."

When Leno at length almost did land a part on a TV series, it came to naught. He was informed that he was too ugly.

Disappointed, but not down for the count, Leno told Mavis, "They are not going to let me in the front door, so I'll have to go around the back. It will just take me longer."

He could only look on in wonder as fellow comedian after fellow comedian scored lucrative, well-publicized deals on TV. Even Letterman won a TV job as early as 1982, while Leno remained a virtual unknown to viewers and labored in obscurity in the boonies—a kind of king of the road.

As luck would have it, Letterman's success likewise contributed to Leno's. When Letterman became the star of the late-night talk show *Late Night with David Lettterman* on NBC, most nights he would invite a fellow comedian on as a guest. Airing at twelve-thirty A.M., the show followed Carson's *Tonight Show*.

Pundits described the wild and wacky show as being "to TV talk shows what Salvador Dali was to traditional painting."

For pranks Letterman would strap a live camera to the back of a chimpanzee and let the animal run wild through the audience, or hold an elevator race in the building, and such antics.

Around this time, Leno was debating what his next move should be to jump-start his disintegrating career. He was firmly stuck in neutral. Then one night Letterman invited Leno onto *Late Night.*

The goofball Letterman hit it off well with the quirky Leno and the audience clamored for more.

Leno confessed, "Dave's show did everything for me. The show is geared well to what I do, in the sense that a lot of jokes I do there wouldn't work on other shows, because the host wouldn't have the rapport I have with David and wouldn't know what I'm talking about."

He went on, "David and I essentially come from the same place, comedically, so we can have a good time."

Comparing his appearance on Carson's show with one on Dave's show, Leno said that he could do things on *Late Night* that he wouldn't dream of doing on Carson's show. "I can be more aggressive on Dave's show than on *The Tonight Show,*" he told the *Boston Herald.* "I can be loud and pick on Dave, really annoy him, which is a lot of fun. Like, when I eat on his show, it drives him crazy. It's *fun* watching him squirm."

Not only did Leno lack the nerve to eat on Carson's show, but he couldn't even work up the courage to call Carson by his first name. It was "Mr. Carson" when Leno addressed the panjandrum of nighttime talk shows. Leno had felt like an unwelcome guest pleading to be on *The Tonight Show.* Mr. Carson, please like my jokes so I can come back again.

The long and the short of it was, Leno simply couldn't kick back and shoot the breeze with Carson the way he could with Letterman.

"When you do Letterman's show," Leno pointed out, "you get recognized by comedy fanatics—college students, and people who go to comedy nightclubs a lot. When you do *The Tonight Show,* you get recognized in the frozen-foods section of the supermarket when you go shopping."

Leno relished trading jokes with Letterman, who was "great from the start, with very clever stuff. Never any cheap shots or Dolly Parton jokes."

Leno, the self-styled "foot soldier of comedy," labeled Letterman "an armchair quarterback." Leno's nice-guy, smiling comic played well against Letterman's surly comic persona. The contrast generated hearty laughs on Letterman's show.

"I have an expression," Leno once said, explaining his gentle image. "Think like a man; smile like a woman. And that's how I get through life. Most people don't know how I feel on most subjects. I don't have a temper. I don't get depressed."

Dennis Miller put it in this manner: "Like Tor Johnson! Nobody knows Leno's back-story. I don't, and I was a decent friend of his. Somewhere along the way, he got hung from a tree by the football team with a massive wedgie—and he went inward."

Not everybody likes Leno's nice-guy personality. Jabbed one critic of Leno, "No interests, no feelings, no soul."

One of Leno's executive producers maintains that Leno's nice-guy image is the real McCoy. "Jay is incredible. He never seems to get tired, is never irritable. Even when he was under extreme pressure he maintained his composure. He's just a really, really nice guy."

But she added in an almost ominous tone: "He's very afraid of *feelings.*"

Time and again his agents would drop him on account of his

niceness. They contended it made his whole personality dull and flat, and as a result of that never managed to reap free publicity.

Such objections always amused Leno. "They thought I was competent enough but not controversial enough. I'd been married to the same person all the time, I didn't drink or do drugs, didn't use obscenities, didn't get thrown out of clubs or fight with producers. They said they wanted to let me go because I wasn't someone whose name would be in the paper on a regular basis.

"It makes me laugh. In February [nineteen ninety-three] there were four hundred eighty-five articles about me and Letterman in the national press."

Earlier in his career, of course, when he was laboring like Sisyphus, he wasn't so amused at the number of articles about him.

Finally, after those exhausting eight years of alienation from *The Tonight Show,* Leno was asked back by Carson to be guest host on his show. The program aired September 6, 1986. As of that date, Jay Leno would cease to appear as merely a guest. From that point on he would always serve as a guest host when he visited the Carson show.

Leno preferred being a host because it was a cakewalk compared to delivering a monologue as a guest. Sure, he got to do his stand-up routine, but for the hosting part, he didn't even bother to read the notes the production staff gave him to prepare for his guests. Leno thought winging it with his guests made for more laughs than simply using the notes themselves.

Carson's *Tonight Show* executive producer, Fred de Cordova, chewed Leno out regularly for his laziness when it came to boning up on his guest interviews. Leno took de Cordova's rebukes in stride.

He had no intention of changing his ad-libbing style of banter into stereotyped boilerplate supplied by the staff researchers.

The year 1986 was a very good one indeed for Leno. Not only did he reappear on *The Tonight Show,* but he played to a standing-room-only crowd at Carnegie Hall in New York City. He went on to host his own sixty-minute special on cable's Showtime. He called it "Jay Leno and the American Dream."

Jeff Jarvis at *People* magazine liked it well enough to give it a "Grade B" at the end of his review. "Though we get plenty of laughs," he wrote, "there aren't as many per minute as there would be if Leno just stood onstage telling jokes." Jarvis compared the Showtime special with Leno's earlier Carnegie Hall show. At Carnegie Hall, Jarvis wrote, "he filled every minute onstage with gags that worked—no groaners, no goofs, no cheap yucks. He's a pro. He's just plain funny."

All in all—a watershed year for Leno. And 1986 wasn't done yet. Next up, he signed a contract for a multiyear deal with NBC for some more specials.

The good news continued to roll in. Johnny Carson selected Leno and Garry Shandling as his two permanent guest hosts for *The Tonight Show.* Shandling quit soon after to star in his own cable program, leaving the whole nine yards to Leno, who couldn't have been happier.

Leno could not figure it out. Why had it taken him so long to achieve a modicum of success?

He decided it must be because "I wasn't 'one of the guys.' When Freddie Prinze did *The Tonight Show,* boom! His first one! Producers called, and he had a series the next day. And a few other people did it that way, too."

He could only shake his head in wonder, trying to dope it out.

"I was dropped from the Morris Agency twice, and from ICM twice. They said, 'There's no future. You have to have a hook. You have to be the guy from outer space or the wacky guy.' But I don't hold any grudge."

Meanwhile, Leno had a ball appearing on Letterman's show playing Wild Man Jay to Letterman's Straight Dave. "I don't think Dave has a mean streak in him. I've never seen him do anything mean. He's just honest. I've just seen him speak his mind. He'll say to a guest, 'Well, that's completely stupid, and you're an idiot.' But he believes that! I believe it, too, but I probably wouldn't *say* it."

For his gigs on *The Tonight Show,* Leno had to tone down his off-the-wall material, because, as he told *Vanity Fair* in 1991, "when I was doing Letterman, the material was a bit more left of center. When you do *The Tonight Show,* you essentially do one-liners about what's gone on that day. And being on once every six weeks with Letterman is different from being on every night of the week [as guest host of *Tonight*].

"And yes, it is more bland now. As I *do* the show now, obviously I'm a guest in somebody else's house. So, you don't criticize. You say, 'Oh, this is fine,' and you work within that framework."

He felt he had a specific chore as a guest host. "I stop and I listen to what people say. I'm not trying to be funny all the time. I don't want to get into the lampshade mentality."

He would calm down after his monologue and become self-effacing as he interviewed his guests, letting them take the spotlight. Being a host was relaxing.

He pointed out, "I don't really have a whole lot of interest in my own career from the standpoint of talking about it. I just ask people questions, the way I do when I'm sitting down at an airport waiting for a plane, something I do a lot."

Above all, he didn't want to hurt anybody's feelings. If he did, he apologized. If a viewer wrote a letter to him criticizing his show, he took the time to answer.

When a woman with an acne-pitted face wrote him a letter objecting to his joke about Central American strongman Manuel Noriega, he phoned her to express his contriteness.

The woman was referring to the joke Leno did holding up a photo of Noriega standing with a wicked-looking machete in his hands. Leno wisecracked, with Noriega's scarred complexion in mind, "Judging by the looks of his face, he's also been shaving with this thing."

Leno explained to the insulted woman, "You know, I was making fun of the *man* and his personality. I didn't mean that he had acne so much as that he was an ugly man." He wasn't about to let the woman think his joke had singled her out for derision, because that wasn't the case.

If there was one thing Leno could not stand it was comics who spewed out invective. Even if it meant critics would consider his jokes tame and colorless, he would not resort to shocking his audience.

"I never thought those shock comedians could last just being antigay or antiwoman. Maybe some of it was funny the first time around, but where do you go from there? Who do you hate the next time?"

The television critic Digby Diehl argued, "Aw, c'mon, Jay. Nobody's asking you to become [Andrew Dice] Clay, but among comedians, don't nice guys finish last?"

Diehl went further: "The great tradition of American humor— from Mark Twain through Will Rogers to Lenny Bruce—has conspired to sting the smug and shake up the complacent. Is Leno becoming too cautious to gore our sacred cows?"

As far as Leno was concerned, why should he tell jokes with an edge to them if he was basically a happy guy? He had nothing to be angry about. He had a good life and he enjoyed it. To come on as the angry young man would be hypocritical of him.

"I have a good family, a good background, a good marriage. So those are the things that most of my humor represents. Now, if a comedian comes from a broken home, had alcoholic parents, or something like that, his or her humor will reflect that. And that's okay with me—as long as it isn't contrived."

Perhaps Diehl had in mind Leno's political jokes, which earlier in his career had had more sting to them than when he became guest host on *The Tonight Show*. In fact, at that time he had made a name for himself in the field of political humor.

Leno came up with six rules for political comedy on *The Tonight Show*, which began to temper his political barbs to some degree.

1. Never do jokes about folks I really don't like. It will come through, and if there's anything that turns people off, it's approaching your material with an attitude.

2. Be careful with physical jokes. The best way to joke about a fat or bald guy is by misdirection. Talk about his lousy taste in ties.

3. There's a way to do ethnic jokes, but the idea is to bring people in, to see things from their perspective. You don't laugh at the stereotype, but the fact that there is a stereotype.

4. As a general rule, no dialect jokes.

5. Make sure your only agenda is humor.

6. First, last, and always, do what the mob does—stay away from the family. Joke about Hillary's health plan, but not about Hillary.

It was by using his nice-guy rules for comedy, such as those above, along with backroom political maneuvering by his manager, Helen Kushnick, that Jay Leno went on to assume Johnny Carson's throne on *The Tonight Show*.

Romance

Her name was Mavis Nicholson and she was trying, valiantly and unsuccessfully, to become a writer of comedy. The writing business, she had found, was one of the hardest to get into on the West Coast, and even with all the pain and the effort it took to do the work, the writer was still the most overlooked person in the whole of show business.

Mavis was trying to get into the joke-writing end of the business, or, perhaps, if that failed, into the sitcom writing business. Everybody wanted to laugh, and actors and writers who were successful at making people laugh became rich and some of them even famous. But so far, she had pretty much failed to make any inroads into the business.

The problem was that she did not know any true comics who

needed material. She had formed several flimsy partnerships with other wannabe writers, but none of these ventures had won her any acclaim—and certainly little if no money. And so she was now on a new leg of her journey toward success. She had decided that she should get acquainted with real working comedians to pitch her material to them.

The Comedy Store was one of her new posts. She came down frequently to take a look at the new comics who were appearing. She knew some night she might find one who would suit her—that is, one she felt she might be able to work for. In addition to that, she knew that the Comedy Store was usually crawling with talent agents looking for comedians to represent and Hollywood producers on the lookout for possible comics they had missed elsewhere. Maybe she would meet one of them to pitch her wares to.

Mavis was a cool, laid-back type of person, having been brought up the daughter of a successful although not well known character actor named Nick Nicholson. But with all that cool, she was shrewd and practical. Besides that, she had a pretty good eye for talent. She was good at picking up-and-coming people out of groups of the "usual suspects."

One night she found herself in the front row, watching with glazed eyes as comic after comic came up to sell their wares. She was spectacularly bored—the quality of the night's comedians was far below average. And then—she revived.

"I was seated front-row center," she recalled, "with my nose practically on the stage, in the middle of this guy's routine. I'd never heard of him, but he was funny, tall, and kind of cute, and after seeing some of the other acts, I realized just how good he was."

There was more. Mavis sat there sizing up this rather personable young man. He was wearing a weird ensemble—even for a comic.

He had on a snap-brim, ace-reporter type of hat out of the Golden Age of newspaper reporter movies, a jeans shirt, a black-leather vest, a huge mother-of-pearl belt buckle, and silly looking wire-rimmed granny glasses.

And then he was gone.

Another comic came on and she began to drowse. When she looked around for the man who had interested her, she could not find him. She simply shrugged it off. Was she interested in him for his comic worth, or was she interested in him as a man? She realized to her embarrassment that it was probably as a man and that she dug him. Her own personal life had suddenly seemed to be headed for the deep six after an affair that had blazed but now seemingly had flickered out—or was on the way to doing so.

She knew there would be other nights, other comics, other men.

And then, as she headed for the rest room before leaving the Comedy Store, she ran right smack into him. He looked at her and she looked at him. Then, when she came out of the rest room, she realized that he was standing there looking at her with a faint smile on his face.

"Say," he said, "you were in the front row." It was a kind of compliment.

"Yeah, that was me," she said, elevating her nose, stiffening her back, and breezing by him as if he were far too unimportant to waste a moment's notice on.

Later, Mavis tried to explain her cold-shoulder reaction. The fact of the matter was that he had caught her by surprise. "When I don't have time to anticipate, I'm shy," Mavis explained. "I also had a boyfriend at the time."

And, even though *that* romance was almost over, it was still in the works.

Nevertheless, she kept kicking herself for not stopping at least for a word or two. She realized he might have been a fun guy in some ways. And so she simply filed away the whole unfinished episode as a lost opportunity.

A week later Mavis visited the Improv, another comedy club in the area, still on the prowl for comedians, talent agents, and/or producers. There was a huge plate glass window across the front of the Improv, through which she could see the crowd inside.

And in the crowd that was milling about she spotted a strange-looking hat and a man's thick black curls that somehow dominated the people around him. As she stared with interest at the scene, he came closer and she saw that the man was smoking a pipe, letting the smoke form huge clouds over the heads of the people. He had hair, she remembered, that most people would die for.

And the man was the same man she had seen the week before.

As she stood there, looking him over again, she realized she would have to do some good detective work to find out exactly who he was. She thought he saw her, but he did not, and simply moved away. Mavis entered the Improv, milling with the crowd, suddenly spotted an old friend in the comic business, and began chatting with her. But her eyes were drifting about the crowd.

Her companion watched her, and the two kept chatting. Quite suddenly the man in the hat and with the pipe emerged from the mass and came up to the two of them. Mavis stared. Her companion said hello, and introduced Jay Leno to Mavis Nicholson.

It was really as simple as that.

The three of them chatted for some time, but finally there were just the two of them—Jay and Mavis. While Mavis did not talk quite as much as Jay Leno did during that conversation, she was thinking a great deal. She was looking him over covertly, and he was having an effect on her.

"I have a tremendous passion for men who have blue eyes, black hair, and large jaws. We were each seeing other people at the time. But Jay was always very supportive. He was like that with everybody—kind, helpful, easy to talk to—but even though we were friends, there was always a little awkwardness, an underlying, unspoken tension between us."

Nevertheless, the tension was of the kind that united rather than separated. Mavis realized that he was an easy person to talk to. She found herself chatting without thinking first what she would like to say. And yet there was really nothing about the conversation that stuck to the ribs—it was mostly throwaway dialogue that acted as a kind of cement for their two psyches.

One fact, however, did emerge. It was that Mavis Nicholson's birthday was September 5. And that fact made a deep impression on Jay Leno.

Leno grew up in a household in which there were a number of women—his mother and his aunts on both his mother's side and his father's side. And he had always collected facts like birth dates. It turned out that after many years of soliciting birth dates from the women he liked the most in his life, with whom he grew up, they were all born in what Leno calls a twenty-four-hour period between September 5 and September 6.

That Mavis was born on September 5 was something Leno could not simply pass over without considerable thought. It was a sure sign of something positive in their relationship.

Leno had always admitted that he had no patience with what he somewhat superciliously called the "dating game."

"I don't drink. I never have." He took no drugs, not even an aspirin. "I remember once Mavis wanted a drink, and the relationship almost degenerated on the spot."

She was annoyed at her "date" for his adamant refusal to get her a drink.

"Look," Leno told her finally, seeing how miffed she was. "Let me give you the money, and you can buy a blouse or something. I don't want to buy you a drink."

He gave her thirty-five dollars.

She bought a blouse.

The incident gave Mavis pause. "I can't tell you how absolutely *peculiar* I thought that was."

From the beginning of their friendship, Mavis and Leno both saw themselves as very different types of people—proving the old adage that opposites *do* attract. In truth, this appearance of opposites might have been only an apparent one.

In a book called *How They Met* (1992), Nancy Cobb described the two of them and the way they both struck her as she viewed them together and conversed with them:

"Mavis and Jay Leno actually sound alike: similar speech patterns, similar timing. With tongue in cheek they approach life hand in glove, a bona fide team. Each is dark, one small, one large; each funny, and each the other's best fan."

Their alikeness was apparently what helped each appreciate the other. Their familiarity with the world of comedy about them certainly did not hurt, either, as they were dating. Neither one of them had any thoughts about marriage at first—which was the typical modus operandi for those times. In fact, Mavis stated it best:

"I was never much interested in marrying. Before Jay, I had

been attracted to a particular type of man: highly neurotic, unre-
lentingly verbal, extremely volatile, hyperemotional. I couldn't even
envision having a relationship with [anyone like Jay] because he was
their polar opposite. Phenomenally stable, completely confident,
with a zero quotient for irritability."

It was her mistaken idea that she would be interested in someone opposite to her—the neurotic volatile type described above.
Whereas she was in fact very much like Jay Leno herself.

"We're two peas in a pod emotionally . . . v-e-r-y s-l-o-w. So it
snuck up on me when I realized one day what had happened. I was
in love with him."

Mavis was quite satisfied to go through life without a husband
or family, simply because it felt all right to her. She looked at it in
a rather romantic way: It was as if there was this marvelous party
going on somewhere in the universe, but she didn't know where it
was, and she didn't know how to get to it.

Then—presto! "One day, I woke up and realized, I'm at the
party. It's Jay. He's the party. He's the destination. And it was the
god-damnedest feeling."

Mavis was a writer, but she had a hard time occasionally getting
the right words to describe how she *felt* about things. She had a
feeling for Leno—she guessed it was love. Then she realized it was
definitely love.

"It was casual at first. We became great friends before we became romantically involved. It took a year before I realized he was
the one. We moved in together."

Their interests were absolutely different. With Jay it was writing
jokes and traveling about telling them. With Mavis, books were the
core of her existence. Her main hobby, aside from reading, was in

collecting books, mostly English and American novels of the late nineteenth and early twentieth century. With Charles Dickens at the top of the list.

Jay, hardly a reader by choice because of his dyslexia problem, was astounded once when Mavis sat down with Tolstoy's *War and Peace*—spending all of a day and a half to pore through it!

Leno's hobby was tinkering with his motorbikes and cars, exactly the opposite of Mavis's interest in intellectual and aesthetic things. The two of them always respected each other's need for plenty of space to work their lives out in. The separate enthusiasms never came to blows with one another.

Jay Leno had never had the slightest intention of trying to change Mavis Nicholson—to make her a biker or something like that. Or make her slow down on her reading. Nor did Mavis ever have any thoughts about trying to change Jay Leno. He would always write his jokes and perform them. Why make him change? And he would always tinker with his engines and motors.

The idea of marriage never seemed to intrude on the happy life of those two lovers for some time after they had moved in with each other. "Oh, I knew you could be happily married," Mavis admitted. "My parents were. But my dad was allowed to be twelve years old forever and my mother was the designated grown-up."

And yet the idea of marriage was always there, lurking in the background. But when they did finally break down and get married, the whole affair resembled one of Jay Leno's routines. He might have orchestrated it as such from the very beginning.

Here are the bare bones of the plot:

Leno knew that Mavis didn't particularly want to get married. Then, one day when Leno was renewing his life insurance, just to be sure he was covered enough in case something happened on one of those flights across the country, or whatever, he noticed that he had a very good policy—one of those comprehensive policies. He was, it turned out, covered for almost any contingency. However, Mavis, who lived with him and shared his life, was not covered for anything.

Legally, as a live-in companion, Mavis couldn't be covered by any of his policies. However, if they were married, the policies could be rewritten and they would both be protected. When he told Mavis about this, she didn't seem particularly interested, since she had never been one to fret about insurance all that much. Eventually she agreed that it might be for the better if they were married.

The upshot of the matter was that they did decide to get married. Leno told his mother about the insurance, and she, with her natural sense of humor, broke down and almost cried. It was the most hilarious thing she had ever heard of—at least the most hilarious *reason* to get married.

"They got married because he had some policy. Mr. Skinflint. Mr. Tightwad."

Finally, in 1980, the two of them were married at the home of Jay Leno's agent and manager, Helen Kushnick, and her husband, Gerold. It was a rather brief but meaningful ceremony—all of six and a half minutes of civil folderol. And so James Douglas Muir Leno and Mavis Nicholson were finally united in marriage forever.

The marriage was as sound as the live-in affair they had conducted before. In searching for the right word that could shed some light on the magic of his marriage, Jay Leno finally came up with the word *narcissism*. You remember Narcissus, the Greek youth who was so beautiful that he fell in love with his reflection in a pond and spent the rest of his life catering to himself and himself only. It's narcissism that could explain why Jay Leno would only see his wife three or four times a week, and why they never planned on having children.

His words: "There's a certain narcissistic appeal in what I do. It's the times we live in. Being funny is an asset. If I lived in the time of Genghis Khan, I wouldn't be doing this. I'd be dead by now. But I have to believe in what I'm doing. You make the product yourself. I work for myself."

He *created* humor. That was his thing in life. "Saying we're in a slow recovery, not a recession, is like saying we don't have any unemployed—we just have a lot of people who are really, really late for work."

Or perhaps the classic Leno gag about oil companies and oil shortages: "Whenever there's one of those bogus shortages, the oil companies give you those stupid brochures, 'Fifty Ways to Save Energy.' They spill eighty million gallons in Alaska, and they want you to go to the bathroom in the dark and save three cents a year."

It was the narcissism that caused Leno to like not only himself but the jokes he came up with. It was the key to his success as a performer *and* as a husband.

With Mavis, it was a little bit different. She had never been in favor of marriage as an institution. Besides, she had never expected to be married. "To me, marriage seemed like the lowest circle of hell. But Jay comes from a traditional family, and I realized that he felt my living with him was less than being married to him."

But she knew one of the keys to the success of their marriage was her husband's legendary niceness. "Jay always goes that extra distance for people." She said that when he was on the road he always called her three times a day. And, of course, she also noted that the enormous, electrified gate in front of their Benedict Canyon mansion in Beverly Hills was not to keep people out. Instead, as

Leno said himself, it was "to keep the starving guard dogs from straying too far off the property."

Early in their marriage, Mavis learned that her father had cancer. "He had no insurance," she noted. "But Jay helped him get the best medical care. At the time nobody in my family, including me, could drive. So nobody but Jay could take my father back and forth to the hospital. And when he had to stay in the hospital, nobody but Jay could take us to visit him."

This went on for three months, with Jay driving the freeways every day. "He barely knew my father, but he never complained, never said he was too tired, never acted as if it was anything at all."

But it did occur to Mavis that it was exceptionally lucky that her husband had no offers for distant gigs during that crucial period.

"Jay never said a word." Then, a long time later, when Mavis was speaking to Jay's manager, Helen Kushnick, she learned the truth. "Helen told me Jay had had lots of offers; he just turned them all down."

Mavis pays little attention to flowers or other gestures of that kind. But what she does pay attention to is the kind of attention Jay paid to her father's illness. "Jay," said Mavis, "delivers with *deeds*."

Dramatics

Although many comedians dream of a career in drama—appearing as real actors in real theatrical enterprises—Jay Leno had never really felt the itch to tread the boards in quite that fashion.

Nevertheless, during the early years of his career—before he attained the enviable status of guest host, and then permanent guest host of *The Tonight Show*—he had taken a flier now and then into the world of acting. This was due almost entirely to the efforts of his ambitious and hard-working manager, Helen Kushnick, who believed that a personality like Leno should try everything within reach in the world of show business—especially if there was money attached to it.

And so, between the years 1975 and 1984, Leno appeared in several of the most popular of the prime-time sitcoms then running, including acting roles in *Laverne & Shirley* and *One Day at a Time.* The difference was that in these roles Leno was *not* Leno, as he was in his guest host chores, but was playing the role of a made-up character to fulfill the plot demands of the sitcom's script.

One of the most durable of the sitcoms of the late seventies and early eighties, *Laverne & Shirley,* revolved around a pair of working-class women involved in coping with the everyday problems of working for a living and being women at the same time. Like its imitators on the scene even today, this sitcom had its roots in an early Broadway hit comedy called *My Sister Eileen.* It was just one of dozens of recyclings and upgradings of the original Ruth McKinney, Joseph Fields, and Jerome Chodorov play of the late nineteen thirties.

Clinging to the vestiges of its root source, the television show was a comic depiction of the lives of two young women, played by Penny Marshall and Cindy Williams. Balanced quite like their original models, the two women were opposites. One was sharp-tongued, shrewd, quick-witted, and defensive. Played by Marshall, she was the leader, much like Eileen's sister, Ruth. Plainer than her roommate, she ran the household and spent much of her time getting her friend out of scrapes, usually romantic ones. The roommate was naive, very trusting, quite pretty, and one of those vulnerable born victims. Played by Cindy Williams, she attracted the lightning just as Eileen always did.

Unlike the Broadway original, which was sophisticated, cosmopolitan, and white-collar to the core, this recycled show was straight blue-collar in tone, with the two women working at a brewery as bottle cappers. Most of the action took place in the apartment, although there were also scenes at the brewery, at bowling alleys and soda fountains. It was fitting that Leno, with his blue-collar orientation and image, should work perfectly in this sitcom. He played Laverne's new boyfriend and, before the episode ended, he had already dumped her and walked off into the night.

"I was mean to Laverne," Leno recalled. As an actor he must have scored big on the reality meter. A few days after the show was aired, Leno was shopping at a supermarket, and a woman he had never seen before approached him and began berating him. She was angry with Leno because of what he had done to Laverne.

"Ma'am," Leno said defensively, "it's the *character* I played. Really—I'm a *friend* of Penny's."

The woman stalked off muttering to herself, never for the moment believing that there was an ounce of truth in what Leno was telling her. She had *seen* what he did to her!

One Day at a Time also ran from 1975 through 1984, starring Bonnie Franklin, Mackenzie Phillips, and Valerie Bertinelli. It concerned a divorced mother and her two teenage daughters attempting to cope with life in the manner of any single-parent family of that time or of now. Although not a total recycling of the original *My Sister Eileen,* this certainly did resemble it, with its two leading stars, its building super, and its associates and boyfriends always passing through.

Again, in *One Day at a Time,* Leno fit in very well with the working-class schemata of the sitcom.

But Kushnick was not getting him acting roles exclusively. During this period she managed to secure him a gig as a guest host for *Friday Night Videos*—which more or less established him as a "guest-host type." The show featured the latest rock-music videos by artists considered the hottest on the musical charts at the time. Included in a wide-ranging mix were videos, profiles of individual stars, and videos of musical numbers they performed. Each show would highlight a World Premiere Video, the first network showing of a major artist's clip.

Friday Night Videos ran from 1983 through the late eighties.

All during this time Kushnick was trying to work out some motion picture deals for her client. It was a difficult transition, of course, from television to film, and things were not going so well. But finally she was able to wangle a job here and there.

In all, Leno made five films. Only in one of these was he listed as a star. In one of the others he was not even *mentioned* on the crawls.

It was way back in 1977 that Jay Leno appeared for the first time on the big screen in an infinitesimally tiny part in *Fun with Dick and Jane.* The Jane in the title had the same name as Jane Fonda, the actress who played the part. Dick, however, was George Segal. Ed McMahon even had a part in the picture. Allen Miller and John Dehner got roles that were mentioned. Leno was not mentioned. Ted Kotcheff directed.

The plot was a lightweight affair concerning George Segal's loss of a job, and his attempts, with his wife, Jane, to cope with a complete loss of income. Of course, they turned to crime—with the usual complications.

Leno never liked his part in this picture, calling it a "don't-blink-your-eyes walk-on."

A year later Leno got a part in a 1978 movie titled *American Hot Wax.* This was a kind of stylized "docudrama," the supposed life of the famous disc jockey Alan Freed. It was "based on fact"— but few facts were evident in the production. Directed by Floyd Mutrux, the picture featured Tim McIntire as Freed, with Fran Drescher, John Lehne, Laraine Newman, Jeff Altman, Chuck Berry,

Jerry Lee Lewis, and Screamin' Jay Hawkins—along with Jay Leno—making up the balance of the cast. Leno even got billing on this one.

He played Freed's chauffeur, and he did the part to a turn with just the proper mixture of snobbery and panache.

In 1978 he got a role as the son of a Mafia don in a picture titled *Silver Bears,* based on Paul Erdman's novel about financial shenanigans in the international silver market. Peter Stone adapted the book for the screen. It had a great cast. It starred Michael Caine, Cybill Shepherd, Louis Jourdan, Martin Balsam, Stephane Audran, Tommy Smothers, David Warner, Charles Gray, and Jay Leno, and was directed by Ivan Passer.

Leno was perfect for the role he played here.

His next appearance was in a film titled *Americathon,* directed in 1979 by Neil Israel. It starred Harvey Korman and John Ritter, along with Nancy Morgan. The cast was an eclectic mix of oddballs including Chief Dan George, Tommy Lasorda, Meat Loaf, and Howard Hesseman. It was narrated by none other than stand-up comedian George Carlin.

Jay Leno's role was that of a prize fighter. His real father at one point in his life had *been* a prize fighter in New York City. Leno did the best he could. So did the rest of the cast. But—

The premise of the script was a good one: For all sorts of imaginary reasons, America was supposedly forced to hold a telethon in order to raise enough money to protect itself from international bankruptcy. The problem for Leno in that role was that he had to box with an old lady who was supposed to be his mother!

It is probably not necessary to record that the picture was a bomb.

In 1987, Leno had his first starring role in a motion picture.

The picture was called *Collision Course,* a so-called culture-clash story involving a Detroit police detective and a Japanese police detective. They are assigned to solve the murder of a Japanese businessman in Detroit.

Pat Morita, the famed *Karate Kid* mentor and former comedian, was already assigned to the role of the Japanese lead. Leno liked the idea of playing opposite Morita, and the filming began—on location in Detroit! Leno was not used to working on location this way. He didn't mind memorizing the lines and doing the retakes required, but it was difficult for him and Kushnick to work in his gigs and hosting jobs during shooting.

"It was a killer," Leno said, "juggling all that stuff. Movies aren't *fun* to make. I'd be on the set and then have to be onstage somewhere at nine-thirty, then have to get back to the location by two in the morning so I could be on the set at six again."

Whew!

The picture was finally in the can, it looked good, and then—

Dino De Laurentiis, who produced, was suddenly in bankruptcy, and all his film products and everything that belonged to him were put on the shelf. Finally, in 1992, just as Jay Leno became the star of *The Tonight Show* after Johnny Carson's departure, the story took another bizarre turn and HBO Video announced that it was releasing the 1987 film on the home video market.

Leno and Kushnick were not necessarily happy about the fact that his first starring role in a film was going to appear on home video, and not on the big screens of America.

"They're just taking advantage of where Jay is now," Kushnick said. "It's so obvious. We had nothing to do with the release of this movie now."

A publicity blitz was unleashed to coincide with Leno's job as host of *The Tonight Show*. Naturally the video did fairly well as a video film exclusively.

The picture was directed by Lewis Teague, and starred Leno and Morita in the leading roles, with Chris Sarandon, Ernie Hudson, John Hancock, Al Waxman, Randall "Tex" Cobb, and Soon-Teck Oh. Leonard Maltin's *Movie and Video Guide 1994* said: "Cops Morita (from Japan) and Leno (from Detroit) link up on a case. Harmless, occasionally funny, instantly forgettable buddy-movie. Leno's only starring role to date."

Joe Bob Briggs of the *Orlando Sentinel Tribune* wrote: "What we have here is the exact same movie as *Red Heat*, only instead of Jim Belushi as a wisecracking Chicago cop, we got Jay as a wise-cracking Detroit cop, and instead of Arnold Schwarzenegger as a humorless Moscow cop, we got Pat as a bumbling Tokyo cop." Briggs gave tongue-in-cheek "Drive-in Academy Award nominations" to Morita, for hiding in a garment bag and saying things like, "Now I tell you whole story" and "You good cop and honorable man," and to Jay for "doing it the drive-in way the first time out."

During the filming of the movie, Leno was visited by a number of reporters for interviews, among them Gene Siskel of the *Chicago Tribune*. With Siskel, he discussed the differences he found between joke-making and film-making.

"It's strange for me to take six months to tell a joke rather than just tell it. We sit around, the cast and I, with the director and the writers, and we keep asking ourselves, 'Is this funny? Is this funny? Is this funny?'

"Earlier today, for example, I thought of a joke I considered pretty good. In the scene Pat and I are together. We confront the bad guys, about six of them, in a warehouse. Pat knocks over some shelving to divert everybody. I grab one of the bad guys."

And Leno says, "You better let us go or we will kill your friend."

To which one of the bad guys says, "Friend?" And instantly blows him away! Leno and Morita duck down out of sight to get away.

"The crew laughed," Leno said. "We put it in. That's the way I work." The crew became Leno's test audience.

But still—to wait six months, maybe even longer, to see if the joke worked. . . .

"It's hard to foretell the proper public reaction. That's why we shoot some scenes two ways. Just for protection. We can decide later in the editing [which one plays]. Also we're not altering the basic structure of the scenes based on the crew; we're just testing some jokes. You can like working with an audience, but basically you still use your own instinct."

Leno had an example for Siskel. "Just the other day I came up with a joke that might be a bit much. I pull out a badge and say, 'Police!' and one of the bad guys pulls out his gun and says, 'Criminal!' " Leno winced at Siskel's expression. "Don't worry, we shot the scene without the gag, too."

Leno had worked out a good idea of his image as it appeared on the screen. He did not want to look either dumb or overbearing—that is, out of character. He made the writers change one scene when his concept was not quite what theirs was.

"They had this scene at the beginning of the movie where I beat up this giant thug—he's played by the humongous Tex Cobb. I said, 'No way. Let's have him beat me up. I mean, I look like a guy who would get beat up.'

"And that's about as deep as I get into acting. I'm not thinking of my character's motivation. It's more like Dean Martin playing

Matt Helm. Actually, I'd rather think of myself more like James Garner, at least in my easygoing manner."

As for films in general, and making them, Leno had this to say: "It's just another brand of [show] business. I'll try anything if people think I can be good at it."

There were drawbacks to filming from the first, of course. "I'd honestly rather have the spontaneity of the audience instead of rehearsing something a dozen times, filming it, and then waiting a good six months to see if it works."

In the end, Leno decided: "Movies are not for me. It may be fun once the movie comes out, but there is no audience for a movie. You do it into space for a camera."

However—

"If the movie's a hit, I'm in good shape. But if it's a bomb. . . ."

Leno had something to say about not only his television appearances, but his film appearances:

"I make my living on the road," he told Siskel. "This TV [and film] stuff is, like, extra. I know it sounds terribly snobby, but I'm just very happy doing what I'm doing."

He hated to watch *Americathon,* one of his earlier films. "What a terrible movie!" On viewing it, he thought it far worse than he had thought when he was working on it.

Of all the pictures mentioned, *American Hot Wax* was a definite success. The studio wanted to remake it as a film-for-television some years after it opened.

"I went over to the studio where they were going to film it and saw a note on the board," Leno said. "They were asking for actors to play the roles in the movie." He tried to laugh at the note on his own role: "We need a Jay Leno type—but *better looking*"!

The Craft of the Joke

It's no easy matter building a joke, and Jay Leno is the first to admit it. There's a great deal of craftsmanship to it, and a great deal of imagination required. Plus that, it takes a lot of rewriting to come up with a good solid joke that makes people laugh.

Jerry Seinfeld has characterized Leno's idea of comedy in this manner:

"One great Leno line is, 'Props—the enemy of wit.' And whenever we're watching someone do a shot on Carson or Letterman, he's always snapping his fingers and going, '*Jokes! Jokes! Jokes!*'

"Because that's his philosophy. You've got to have a steady rhythm of jokes that you can snap your fingers to. It's not so much that you understand the lyrics, but it's got to be good to dance to.

Ultimately he wants everyone to do exactly as he does—only less well."

Leno goes through variations of jokes, seeing which one of them sounds best:

"You've really got to structure jokes the way you would a book or a sentence. If I said *car* two jokes ago, I'll say *automobile* this time around, or *vehicle*—just to keep that meter. It has to be interesting-sounding, as well as being funny. I really go over each word, and I say, 'There's one too many words in this sentence. What can I take out? What can I add?' Because the trick is to get to the punch line as quickly as possible. That's the whole thing in comedy.

"You try to work with a formula. For example, they've got this stupid TV show called *Finder of Lost Loves*. Now I've got a couple different ways to approach it. I was going to approach it from the way of, 'You know, it's amazing. Here we are in this country, and we can't get the FBI to set up a hot line for runaway children, but we have a police force to find a girl I used to go out with.'

"I may either do it that way or from the standpoint of, 'Gee— that girl that threw up in my car. I wonder what happened to her? I'd like to find her.'

"I'll try it a number of ways before I see which one works best. I'll spend the next three or four days putting that line together."

He gave another example of his joke-writing technique to Graydon Carter of *Rolling Stone* magazine during an Atlantic City gig.

As Leno perused an index card with a joke written on it, he told Carter, "I'm trying to decide. A couple—where is it? Tennessee. A couple in Tennessee are getting divorced and are arguing about their frozen embryos. And I say, 'You know what's bad? How about the kids? It's hard enough to accept the fact that you're adopted. But now you're defrosted. You're adopted *and* defrosted.' "

That turned out to be a first draft of the joke, which mutated into another version as Leno prepared for his act in his dressing room. Now the joke read:

"It's tough enough finding out you're adopted. Now you find out you're defrosted. A Tennessee couple are divorcing and they're arguing over who gets the frozen embryos. And you thought dividing up the record albums would be tough!"

Still not good enough for Leno's taste. It needed work. He continued to tinker with it, rewriting it till it was as funny as he could get it. The joke, in its polished form, appeared on *The Tonight Show* as:

"This is kind of sad. Have you heard about this couple in New Jersey that are getting a divorce and they're fighting over custody of their frozen embryos? See, I feel sorry for the frozen embryos. You know, it's tough enough when you're a kid growing up and later finding out you're adopted, but to find out you've been *defrosted* . . . !"

For some reason, Leno had decided the state of New Jersey was funnier than that of Tennessee—or was New Jersey the actual state? In the final form of the joke the key word had become *defrosted,* whereas in the joke's previous incarnation Leno was keying on the phrase "dividing up the record albums"—which isn't as funny.

The third version of the joke is more closely akin to the first—in the use of the word *defrosted* in the punch line—than it is to the second, and the final version is snappier.

Here's another joke Leno worked on for hours till he got it down pat:

"They say you're safer in the air than you are in your own bathroom. But I never slipped on the toilet and fell thirty-five thousand feet. I never moved the shower curtain and had a fireball come out and incinerate me."

He stays away from jokes about people he feels strongly about, such as Michael Milken, who did time for his Wall Street junk-bond swindles, because he finds certain people too revolting to make jokes about. Milken makes real-estate wheeler and dealer Donald Trump look like an angel. "At least Trump employs people; at least he builds something," remarked Leno.

Even Colonel Qaddafi looks good compared to Milken. "Qaddafi's a madman, but at least he built hospitals." Just about everyone is better than Milken. "Even Bolivian drug dealers give something back to the community."

His attention to crafting the perfect joke has opened Leno up to the accusation that he is a technician rather than a conceptual comedian.

Leno responded to the criticism in *Philadelphia* magazine: "I don't mind if someone says I'm a technician. If they say nobody laughs, *then* I want to know why. The idea is to pack as many jokes into an area as you can. You try to do what people like, and not what you like."

He added, "There's an old saying. When the band laughs, you're out of show business."

The later at night he appears in front of an audience, the more conceptual Leno becomes. "If it's late at night, and the crowd is kind of hip, then I can get conceptual."

He tells different jokes for different crowds because crowds react differently to the same joke.

"But say, whenever I have a large Oriental audience, I tell them, 'I was watching *Bonanza,* you know, Hop Sing [the Cartwights' Chinese manservant]. . . . Why is it whenever a person of Asian descent enters, the producer feels the need to do that stupid melody: "Ling-ding?" They don't do this for white people: When Clint Eastwood comes on, they don't play "How Much Is That Doggie in the Window?" ' When I do that, Oriental people come up after the show and say, 'Oh, you know, my father, he gets mad when they do that on TV!' "

Leno blasted the modern political humor that he considers racist. "Or like what passes for political humor now. These morning deejays, they say these racist things. I was in Dallas—it was Martin Luther King's birthday—and some deejay said something about, 'If they shot two more, we'd get the whole week off.' And this was considered outrageous—it's not. It's just *racist*."

And the same holds true for antiwomen jokes. "It's the same thing with the way they treat women. In fact, the only shows I really don't like are all-men shows, when they expect you to be really stupid or vulgar. I just don't do that kind of stuff. My mom was a big influence. I genuinely like women. You watch comedians now: Marriage always stinks, no one ever makes love after marriage. Just by being reasonably egalitarian, I get more women who come up and thank me for not doing bimbo jokes or 'my wife' jokes. It's so stupid!"

In fact, one night when shock jock Howard Stern appeared on Leno's show in 1996, Leno apologized to the audience for Stern's tacky behavior. He had brought two buxom blondes in pink bikinis with him. He later proceeded to slap the all but naked behind of one of the blondes right in front of Leno's face, as though he were slapping out a musical riff. Leno found the antic distasteful and degrading, in no way funny.

* * *

Leno has been known to inject a bad joke deliberately into a routine, aiming for the joke to bomb so he can react humorously to the crowd's negative reception. In other words, it's a case of setting up the crowd in advance for a payoff reaction.

For example, referring to the *Exxon Valdez* oil spill off the Alaskan coast, he quipped, "Exxon's got a new promotion going now. With every fill-up, you get a set of drinking glasses depicting all the wildlife they've killed."

Leno analyzed the joke thus: "It's a real hard joke. You are conjuring up an image that people don't want to hear. Oh, gee! You think of the ducks and the otters—just dying—and oh, it's not a comfortable thing for people to think of."

Knowing full well the joke would elicit groans, Leno had a second joke up his sleeve. "So when they go, 'Ooooohhh,' then I can scream and go, 'Oh! It's my fault . . . yell at me!' "

Even as he was preparing the *Valdez* material, doubts lingered in his mind that the subject matter might be too painfully rough to evoke a laugh. "That night I kept saying to myself, Jesus, is this Exxon stuff going to be too harsh? Well, I realize now it wasn't. In fact, the next week I was able to step it up a little and see what the mood of the country was then."

Since each audience is different, Leno likewise recasts each joke a tad here, a tad there to suit the particular audience's taste—at least he did when he was on the road a lot before settling in as permanent host of *The Tonight Show,* with only a few road dates to fuss with. Ever the craftsman, he senses the nuances of distinction that inform an audience.

"When you're doing a college, you can talk about the neo-Nazi fascists at the phone company, and when you do a Perry Como show, you'd say, 'Those crazy people at the phone company are unbelievable.' "

Leno once revealed this in-depth dissection of one of his protean jokes:

"I had this joke about going to Europe and walking into the Vatican gift shop, where I found the same crummy stuff you see everywhere—you know, the 'Where's the Beef?' T-shirts, and so forth.

"But I found that if I said that I went to Europe, I got something negative from the crowd. Because, of course, most of them do not go to Europe. It was as though I had distanced myself from them.

"People said to me, 'Go on: do the joke anyway.' I said, 'No, I can feel it. It's like they think I'm trying to show off. Like I'm name-dropping or something.' "

It finally occurred to him on a trip to Europe in 1984 how to retool the joke so that it would not distance him from the audience. By bonding with the audience and making the joke accessible to them he would be able to crack them up.

He changed the opening line to, "Hey, I bought my ticket to heaven—I took my parents to Europe."

Now that he had introduced his parents into the joke, the audience warmed toward him, thinking, Isn't that nice?

One of Leno's mottoes for joke telling is, "When you're a comedian, you have to be similar enough [to the audience] to share experiences." For him that means steering clear of cocaine jokes because, "You know, most people don't do cocaine. I don't do cocaine."

Do a Gary Hart joke instead:

"I was on a plane the other day and Gary Hart sat across the aisle. And it was so strange: Here's a man who almost got to be president of the United States, and my wife walks by him and says to me, 'Oh, I hope he doesn't grab my ass.'"

Another hobbyhorse of Leno's is lampooning hypocrites. "Americans do have a good sense of fair play. And hypocrisy is a great target for comedians. People can get away with anything, except just don't be a hypocrite about it. That's the number-one thing."

He believes comedy is "instinctual." "I have no interest in *thinking* about it. I have no books about comedy. Walk around my house, you'd have a hard time figuring out what I do for a living. You'd probably think I was a mechanic, because I have so many car books. I don't have masks of comedy and tragedy, or Ed Wynn's hat on a hook. When you start *thinking* about comedy, you become a humorist or a satirist, and eventually you're out of business."

He contends that simply saying certain words elicits laughter. He labels them "punch words"—such as *Donna Summer, discos,* and *Harvey Wallbanger.* He really doesn't know why. "People just react to them with a laugh."

It is important to be consistent when relating a joke, Leno maintains. "A lot of times when I used to go to the Catskills I'd watch neophyte comedians—guys in their early twenties. In the beginning of their act, their wife is fat and ugly and awful to sleep with, and then, eight jokes later, they've got a gag about how their wife's a nympho. 'Make up your mind!' I'm thinking. 'Where are you coming from?' Early on, I decided to make sure that my stuff sticks to what I am or what my point of view is."

High-concept comedians draw crowds that fill the theaters,

which is exactly what Leno wants to do—and does. "If I were not a mainstream comedian, most places would be only about half-full. You have a lot of people out there over the age of fifty, and you have a lot of people under the age of thirty. In this economy, you're not going to attract all of the people in either one of those groups. So you need *everybody*."

He went further, explaining how he keeps his theaters packed. "I was once asked why I was afraid to tick off my audience. They're my audience! Why would I *want* to tick them off? I just don't understand the logic there. To me, if you're a comedian, you should make everybody laugh. Everybody. Case closed."

It's especially important not to tick off certain people. At one gig he spotted a guy in the audience who was wearing a goofy hat. Deciding to ridicule the hat, Leno asked the guy who he was. "I run this place," was the answer. Leno ad-libbed on the nail. "Well, that's an excellent hat, sir. And a fine, fine head."

On a slightly different note, Leno turned disaster to victory one night during the middle of an interview. "I had a little kid on, a precocious three-year-old from a TV show. He said he was learning the alphabet, so I drew an N and said, 'What letter is that?' He went, 'Z.' The audience went, 'Aww. . . . ' I turned the paper— 'Oh, right, it is a Z,'—the audience went, 'Ooooooh!' and the kid was proud of himself. That was my favorite ad lib. I thought, 'This is fun; I like doing this.' "

Adapting to each audience is second nature to Leno. It's a sixth sense he developed to survive in the comedy jungle. "I opened for Perry Como on a summer tour once. There was no way I was going to get away with a lot of blue material. I was glad that I could work to that audience." And again he emphasizes, "A comedian should be able to make *everybody* laugh."

To achieve this elusive goal, he rewrites a joke until he's blue in the face, simply to get a winner like this one: "President Reagan has now come out against the electric chair. He feels there are now so many men on death row, he would like to have electric bleachers."

This "simple joke," as Leno calls it, went through a plethora of variations and reconstructions to become an uncomplicated joke. It's like what Hemingway used to say about a good short story— that is was like an iceberg, with most of it out of sight.

Leno parsed the joke in the following fashion:

Have you heard this? President Reagan has now come out against the electric chair.

"People will listen," says Leno, "because they know that's contrary to what he believes—or at least what he is thought to believe. 'Ooooh!' says the audience."

He feels there are now so many men on death row—"This is a thoroughly logical reason to back up the president's purported change of mind."—*he would like to have electric bleachers.*

Leno expounds why the punch line works. "Instead of just an electric chair, the president opts for many chairs—'bleachers.' The fact that the word *bleachers* usually refers to an audience and not the victim of the chair makes no difference. The word *bleachers* immediately reaffirms what the audience already thinks about Reagan."

And you thought writing a joke was easy.

While inventing a good joke, Leno must try to avoid outthinking the audience. If the joke is too complex or too arcane, the audience won't get it.

Such a joke is this one: "Recording star James Brown served only six months of his six-year sentence, and now I understand John Poindexter is taking singing and dancing lessons."

Waiting for gales of laughter from the audience when he told the joke, Leno stood nonplussed in a stony silence. The joke was beyond their grasp. They had no idea who John Poindexter was. Or maybe they didn't know that Brown was a famous singer. Whatever, the joke bombed, and Leno moved on to the next one chop-chop.

To avoid incomprehensible jokes, Leno as guest host used to invite a knot of fellow comics to his house to try out the jokes on them before doing his stand-up on *The Tonight Show*. Going over his material, Leno would ask his buddies which jokes work and which should be cashiered from his act. Scarfing down hamburgers and pizza, the comedians have a great time whittling down the number of jokes to twenty-five gems. What better way to spend an evening than laughing the whole night away?

To obtain the requisite twenty-five jokes, Leno would start out with about fifty or sixty gags that he has worked on during the day. Sometimes the number was closer to a hundred or a hundred and fifty. It all depended.

The structure of his monologues has remained pretty much the same from the start after taking over from Carson. The opening joke is the big story of the day, succeeded by lesser-known stories. The only time he does not adhere to this structure is if the headline story of the day is too tragic to make light of, in which case he starts with the next newsworthy story—preferably a topic that hasn't appeared in the news before.

"You open with a few jokes about whatever the big story of the day is. And then, as you move through it, you get to the lesser stories. Then maybe there are a couple of jokes about social issues—you know, like 'Dear Abby'—or a sports joke. Then near the end of the monologue, you tend to do more jokes about entertainment, about commercials, or about television shows."

One reason Leno is so intent on performing good jokes is because he doesn't "die" well onstage, unlike Johnny Carson, who often was at his funniest when his jokes bombed and, dying, he had to save his neck onstage by ad-libbing. Leno's only defense if his joke flops is to move on pronto to the next one.

This rapid shuttling to the next joke has caused certain critics to charge that Leno is out of touch with the audience because he does not respond to their negative reactions to a joke. Whether his joke bombs or succeeds, Leno giggles, although he does it somewhat less than he used to, and then presents the next joke. His rapid-fire progress from joke to joke makes it difficult for the audience, especially the TV audience, to know if the live audience laughs are for the joke he's currently telling or are residual laughs from the previous joke he told.

Leno explained to Mary Billard of *Gentlemen's Quarterly* how he arrived at a joke comparing the captain of the *Exxon Valdez* to Otis, the bloodhound-faced wino on the old *Andy Griffith Show*.

The very image of Otis tickled Leno's funny bone. That was how the joke started. "Right away," said Leno, "Otis conjures up an image of a heavy-set guy who hasn't shaved."

Originally, Leno had wanted to incorporate the pun "half-baked Alaska" into the joke, but it was too lame and uninspired.

Then Leno wanted to change the setting of the joke from the coast of Alaska to another waterway. "I tried the Strait of Hormuz, but that didn't sound good. I tried the Cape of Good Hope. There aren't many people who know those are the worst waters in the world, you know, trying to get around the Cape."

That didn't work either. No watery setting came to mind, so he pared the joke down to the bare-bones image of a juicehead captain negotiating treacherous seas with weaving ten-mile turns.

Performing the joke on TV, he choreographed it, mimicking Otis's intoxicated efforts to steer the pitching ship. "Oh, look out, look out—*wow*!"

The thing about comedy is, it doesn't change over the years, according to Leno. "Comedy's pretty constant. . . . The same things that are funny now have always been funny. If you watch the Keystone Kops or Keaton or Chaplin, you'll see they hold up very well because nothing has changed. I don't think any differently than Alan King did. I don't take his jokes, but I use the same mock outrage, the same annoyance at things. Good comedy isn't doing things differently, it's doing the same things better."

Leno favors blue-collar jokes. "Not from the point of being dirty, but from the point of being stuff that everybody can understand."

Take Leno's Yugo jokes, for example. Everyone can relate to the ill-fated Yugo. "A new antitheft device is to make the name larger," said Leno. At another time he quipped, "And Yugo had trouble passing the crash test. You know, they couldn't get the dummy to go in the car."

McDonald's is always a good subject for Leno to poke fun at. "McDonald's has the McRib sandwich—they're determined to use every part of that cow. What's next? The McCowhead?"

Leno believes people prefer jokes about politicians to ones about corporations because "I find people are more frightened by jokes about corporations than any kind of political joke. If I do jokes about Bush and Quayle, especially Quayle, they laugh, no matter how tame the joke.

"Sometimes I'll say, 'Oh, stop. It's not even that funny.' I did one about him last week. I said, 'It was Marilyn Quayle's birthday, and Dan took her to her favorite restaurant—Chuck E Cheese.' They go, 'Whooooo!' 'It's not that funny! Now stop it!' I say. But you make fun of McDonald's or anything thought to be a corporate sponsor, and people will go, '*Ooooo*.' I think they think you've gotten yourself in trouble."

Nevertheless, Leno continues to make jokes at corporations' expense.

"See what Arco has done? They've combined the all-night minimarket with the twenty-four-hour gas station to try to give you a one-stop robbery center. This way criminals don't have to drive around all night wasting gas. You pull in at nine-fifteen, shoot the attendant, and you're in bed by eleven."

Not only Arco takes it lumps from Leno:

"Been to your local Mobil station lately? The station's owned and operated by Abdul Yashima. Guys are cooking dogs in the work bay. They're having a holy war with the Iraqi Chevron station down the street."

He likes deriding airlines, too.

"They say flying is safer than walking. When was the last time you saw an insurance machine in a shoe store?" and, "I always get stuck in the middle seat, between the screaming baby with diarrhea and the octogenarian with halitosis. We're like the three ages of man winging through time."

Politicians remain Leno's favorite target, such as Mayor Richard M. Daley.

"Most people who voted for his father are dead," cracked Leno. "Then again, most of them were dead when they voted for his father."

Back to George Bush. Recalling the incident when Bush was vice president and a toddler called Jessica McClure fell into a well in Texas, Leno said, "She was doing fine, but what an ordeal! In the well for fifty-eight hours—and then having to meet George Bush! It's enough to make her want to go back down."

The former Soviet Union wasn't safe from Leno's gibes:

"The vegetables are moldy, the meat is rancid, yet they keep their leaders fresh and crispy."

When Gorbachev met Fidel Castro in 1989, Leno wised off, "He was cheered by ten thousand screaming Cubans. That was over Miami."

Leno considers his comedy funny because it "comes from reality." People used to laugh at ethnic jokes because they were uneasy or afraid of the unknown. Now they groan at ethnic stuff.

"Today's audiences are uneasy about high tech, nuclear war, and computers—the unknown—that's what they laugh at, the human spirit overcoming the technological age.

"They have to know where you're coming from, and they don't want to hear something they've heard before."

His closeness to reality enables him to joke about the recession. "I heard an economist on the news tonight. He said the recession is over. I guess he sold his house."

* * *

Family comedy is a favorite with the G-rated Leno. He has joked about the time he bought his mother a remote control TV. Months later when he visited her, he discovered the remote control squirreled away in a drawer.

"I was afraid to start a fire," said his mother.

Leno joked to the audience, "She thinks it throws electric sparks across the room."

About his father, Leno jested, "He won't get a hearing aid. He just figures if only Tom Brokaw and Peter Jennings would stop mumbling. When I drive to their house, I can hear the TV five exits away."

Practically every time Leno opens his mouth another anecdote pops out. Slices of life turn into instant comedy routines—he calls then riffs—through the alchemy of his mind, never mind what's made up or what isn't. It's the anecdote as it exists that counts.

Example:

One day recently Leno pulled onto the shoulder of the freeway to aid motorists whose car had broken down. They were huddled around an old Caddy, wondering how to get it started. Leno handed them his car phone so they could call for help. The men beamed happily and phoned home, handing the phone back to Leno, who went off feeling he had done his good deed for the day.

Later he got the phone bill. The stranded motorists had called home—and home was in El Salvador!

Occasionally, Leno will take a potshot at a touchy subject in his comedy routines, such as the homeless. "They get two meals, one at Thanksgiving and one at Christmas. Then it's, 'Hey, pal, you can't eat now, it's only July.' "

Then it's back to family jokes, such as one about his wife. "My wife's from here [L.A.], and not only is her high school gone, but the hill her high school was on is gone! But there are advantages to L.A. You can get *People* magazine here on Sunday. In Andover, they don't get it until Thursday."

Leno's love of family jokes can be traced back to his love of family.

"My grandfather was an Italian immigrant," he has said. "I always felt that restlessness to be somewhere else. Back East I'm that crazy comedian from California, but here [in California] I'm the straightest guy in the world. I don't smoke or drink or do drugs. Maybe it's an inferiority thing with my older brother, who went to Yale and was one of the ten smartest students in the country.

"I have an adventurous spirit. It's one of the things that makes the West Coast different from the East Coast. My dad was in his fifties before we could really talk. He was a child of the Depression. I guess I've inherited the fear of being broke."

For Leno, comedy is conservative, not liberal. "One of my favorite subjects in comedy is injustice, but I think rebellion is funniest when it comes from within the system. Comedy is essentially conservative. You need to come from a conservative background. Take someone like Sam Kinison. For his stuff on marriage to be funny, he had to set it up in a conservative way, like: 'I was married. We had a little house. We had an idyllic thing.' He'd set it up that way, and then go into a rant."

Leno prefers "guys who don't do shtick, such as Bob Newhart or Robert Klein—that's the kind of stuff I want to do."

In the name of comedy, Leno will also make fun of himself. "I got a two-page spread in *Newsweek*. I called my buddies back home." Then the punch line: "They don't get *Newsweek*."

Unlike Carson, Leno doesn't like editing jokes from his monologue as he's delivering it. Carson used to have his cue cards lined up in a row in front of him as he performed. If he didn't like a joke, he skipped it and went on to the next.

Leno utilizes a single cue-card man who holds all his jokes in a pile so that Leno can only see the one on top. That way Leno can't skip any of the jokes, which constrains him to follow the logical progression of the jokes no matter how the audience reacts.

"I do them this way because then I have to do the joke. That's just my own personal thing. If the monologue isn't doing well, I can't bail. Because I have to do this joke to get to that joke. You go out there and you do the joke. And I figure if I'm going to stay up all night putting these jokes together, I should at least do them."

The comedians who have always cracked Leno up are Johnny Carson, David Letterman, Jerry Seinfeld, Steve Wright, Carol Leifer, Elayne Boosler, and of course, Klein and Newhart. "I like people who use words effectively," Leno said. "I don't like the 'pie-in-the-face' comedians."

When Leno really feels adventurous he'll do a drug joke, but it won't have anything to do with his personal experience. It will usually have to do with the political situation relating to drugs. In fact, you would be just as accurate to call it a political joke as to call it a drug joke.

Or in the following instance you could even call it a corporate-political joke:

"A lot of people in Colombia feel that Americans have no right to go down there and interfere. But Americans think, 'Sure we do, because in America, the customer is always right.' "

The Colombian joke is a near cousin to Leno's corporate jokes like, "They want us to call Kentucky Fried Chicken KFC now. Why not call it CPR, or DOA?"

He enjoys mocking celebrities, which fits in well with his news-oriented monologues. Isn't it always the politicians and the celebrities who get all the play in the media?

Re John McEnroe: "A plane crashed in John McEnroe's backyard a few years ago. It's true. Well, McEnroe *says* it was in his yard. Officials say it was . . . on the line."

Old Blue Eyes comes in for his share of comedic abuse as well. "Frank Sinatra is such a big star that when he plays Las Vegas, all they've got to put on the marquee is 'Frank,' and everybody knows who they're talking about. Jerry Lewis is so big in France that when he's there, the ads simply say, 'The King Is Back.'

"I'm so big in Japan, they don't put anything in the paper. People open the paper, they don't see my name—they know I'm in town, and they rush to the club."

Actually that was a joke at Leno's own expense, but the name of Sinatra grabbed the audience's attention. Leno had no reluctance to name-drop if it'll prick up the audience's ears.

Then it's back to tried-and-true airline jokes, e.g., the rubbery chicken served on board. "The stewardess said, 'You can have either the sirloin steak or tapioca chicken.' I never heard of tapioca chicken!"

Or this one about a ramshackle airline, which shall remain nameless:

"It was like stepping into the hold of some kind of flying slave ship. The flight attendant was Helga the stomping mare, wearing a Mayan death mask."

Leno likes telling unique jokes that don't come ordinarily to mind. "I'm tricky to write for. I tend to be more cerebral, and not so obvious." Out of a thousand jokes mailed to him, he'll select ten or less as a matter of course. If he uses the sender's joke, he'll pay him fifty bucks.

He once told his audience about an article he had read that said that most airplane accidents took place not in the air but on the ground. Taken aback, Leno said, "Of course, it's not until you hit the ground that you experience that minor discomfort."

On occasion Leno will tell jokes about ordinary joes, as opposed to politicians and celebrities. He once told this joke about the security guards who patrol *The Tonight Show* soundstage:

"Security guys are the ones who know least about what's going on. At NBC there was a guy who stopped me and said, 'Who're you?'

" 'Jay Leno,' I said. 'I'm hosting *The Tonight Show*.'

" 'Right,' the guy says. 'Johnny Carson hosts *The Tonight Show*.'

" 'I'm subbing for him.'

" 'Right. So what's your name?' The guy picks up the phone and says, 'I have a Jim Reynolds here who says he's hosting *The Tonight Show*.'

" 'It's not Jim Reynolds. It's Jay Leno. Jay!' Jeez."

Then it's back to celebrities, like Liberace. "I've got to show you this old magazine I just bought. It's got an article by Liberace called 'What I Want in a Woman.' "

Or Lee Iacocca.

"Lee Iacocca has turned down the Pennsylvania governor's invitation to fill a vacant seat in the U.S. Senate. I think he did the right thing. Do we really need a senator whose slogan is: 'If you can find a better politician, buy him'?"

Of course this joke won't fly if the audience doesn't have the requisite intelligence to know that at the time of the joke Iacocca was the chairman of Chrysler, which used to run the catchy ad, "If you can find a better car, buy it."

Sometimes Leno's jokes earn him enemies. Certain celebrities don't like to be ridiculed and will make a stink about it to Leno. When he poked fun at Roseanne's weight during one of his monologues, Roseanne had a cow. Seeing him at the Improv, she called him onto the carpet for his tasteless lack of consideration for her feelings.

This came as a surprise to Leno, who thought it was okay to kid her about her weight problem because she herself had made jokes about it on her HBO special, in which she said something to the effect that "we fat people have to stick together." She objected to his material on the grounds that that did not give him the right to humiliate her on account of her weight. She didn't want to hear about her being fat anymore. Enough was enough.

All tact, nice-guy Leno agreed never to joke about her obesity again. And he kept his word.

As a rule most celebrities don't complain to Leno when made a butt of his jokes. If they did, Gentle Jay would soon be out of a job, as celebrities always come in for a raft of lampooning in his monologues. And they always will.

eizing the Throne

If 1986 was the watershed year for Jay Leno's career, then 1991 would have to be called the year of consolidation. Since moving to the West Coast in 1974, he had continued to hone his comedic talents to a razor-sharp edge. And he had pretty well perfected the stand-up style he wanted to use in his future years as a comic.

Most of his time on the Left Coast had been spent commuting to somewhere else, as far as his three-hundred-odd gigs a year were concerned. He had fine-tuned himself into a joke machine that could go into any bar, nightclub, convention center, auditorium, or theater and deliver off the top of his head an appreciative, happily amused audience. *Anywhere*—without exception.

By the early 1990s he had worked out a variety of levels for his jokes. By sizing up an audience in a shrewd minute or so at the start, he could deliver the rest immediately right on target. But of course there were those jokes that *did* fail—and when they did, Leno would come up with what he came to call a "condom-Geraldo" joke, in other words, a surefire *slightly* off-color gag destined to elicit laughs in any audience.

These were risqué jokes, yes, but not the X-rated type. After all, Leno never did do blue jokes, since they did not tally with his well-crafted, nice-guy, rather old-fashioned image.

The slightly racy joke was tailored to his clean-cut image so that it would reach the largest number of people while offending as few of them as possible.

He was more comfortable, of course, with clean material. "I find it more interesting, and more challenging, to try to write something that's clean and funny and appeals to everybody."

He has made it a practice to adhere to his so-called thirty-nine-and-a-half rule. According to this rule, when a woman watches a guy in his twenties cracking dirty jokes onstage, she giggles and thinks he's a sexy hunk. "Oh, I can't *believe* he said that. Hee, hee!" But when the same woman watches a thirty-nine-and-a-half-year-old comic trying the same jokes, she finds him disgusting, what with his receding hairline and beer belly slopping over his belt. "Oooooh! That *old* guy. He's really *gross!*"

One of Leno's condom-Geraldo jokes might be the one he told about Ted Kennedy. "People laugh at Ted Kennedy, but how many other fifty-nine-year-old men do you know who still go to Florida for spring break?"

A tad off color, but certainly not blue.

His job as a comedian is, as he sees it, "to kind of degrade and humiliate the whole system fairly equally."

Some of his Washington jokes are his favorites. "I've worked a number of clubs there, but my impression? It's like they say, politics is show business for ugly people. Washington is like Hollywood—the motives and goals remain the same, but the people aren't nearly as attractive."

Another favorite: "On the news they showed Ford, Carter, Bush, and Clinton all standing together. It looked like a police lineup for who killed the economy."

Not all of his jokes worked. He once told national correspondent Victor Gold of the *Washingtonian Magazine* a joke that he thought was good, which drew the following reaction:

"It's strange that Clinton is using huge props to get his point across. In November, you're electing Thomas Jefferson. In September you wind up with Gallagher."

"Gallagher?" asked Gold.

"You know, Gallagher the prop comedian. . . . Yeah, well, maybe that's a little inside."

Leno likes politicians who have a sense of humor. "I think Dole has a good sense of humor. And I think Bill Clinton does, too. And Al Gore—we've done things with him on the phone, and he's very funny, a real good sport. But you know, having a sense of humor and being able to tell a joke are two different things. The ability to laugh at yourself and have a good time with it, that's what's important."

Stephen Saunders, whose job was to monitor TV for the "White House Bulletin," a daily news service reporting on current events in Washington, admired Leno's political barbs. "He's more on top of the day's issues and events than his competition. I'd say Leno is even better than Carson in using one-liners to define the issues Joe Six-Pack thinks about—not only the issues, but the political personalities."

Leno feels the key to the success of his political gibes is his refusal to side with either party. "The key to doing political humor on *The Tonight Show* is for people not to know how you feel politically. And not to get personal—you know what I mean? I once saw a comedian do a whole bit about Reagan's neck, how it looked like a turkey's, and I told him afterwards, 'That's not a political joke—a person can't help the fact that he's old. Go after what he says and does—that's political humor.' "

When people charge that he is out to "get" Clinton, it puzzles him. "Well, that kind of makes me laugh because I used to get all these letters saying, 'You're a Democrat because you do all those Bush-Quayle jokes to get Clinton elected.' Now I get letters, 'You're a Republican and you're out to ruin Bill Clinton.' "

What those accusers didn't understand is that Leno feels this way: "You go after whoever's in power. Like when we do jokes about Hillary, it's because she's in a place of power, not because she's a woman. Sometimes I'll watch male comedians and they'll do jokes that get personal, sort of crude. That sort of thing turns people off."

It is Leno's belief that people want political humor like the following: "Some people think that April Fools' Day is kind of silly. Taking one day out of the year to honor the vice president—I don't think that's too much."

He explained, "You really have to put yourself in the place of the people in the audience" to be a successful comedian. "If I see someone who's not laughing, my instinct isn't to get annoyed—it's to figure out why they don't understand. Sometimes it's not that someone's dumb, it's just that they're not educated.

"Now, with college today, you have the brightest crowds, but

Jay may want to forget this appearance in *Silver Bears,* one of his inauspicious roles in film. He is shown here with, from left, Cybill Shepard, Michael Caine, Louis Jourdan, Stephane Audran, and Tony Mascia, in 1977.

In the past, Jay's comedian friends teased him for being fashionably challenged because of outfits like this one.

The easy camaraderie between Jay and David Letterman, pictured here in 1986, became a fierce competition when their two shows went head to head.

Jay has looked up to Johnny Carson as both a friend and a mentor during much of his career.

After he was hired to take the helm of the *The Tonight Show,* Jay underwent a startling transformation from a wacky stand-up comedian to a polished interviewer and host.

Jay is shown below performing at the Improv, a legendary Los Angeles comedy club. His friend Jerry Seinfeld has referred to him as "Robo-comic" because of Jay's seemingly endless number of stand-up appearances.

As host of *The Tonight Show,* Jay always rises to the occasion, whether it is with Apple, the dog who swallowed a knife, or with the cast of *Cheers* at the final *Cheers* episode party in Boston.

Jay has proved to be an adept interviewer of guests ranging from Tom Brokaw to Howard Stern.

An avid collector of automobiles and motorcycles, Jay has extensive collections of both.

Jay and his wife, Mavis, seen here at the Emmy awards in 1994, have a home in Beverly Hills.

In July 1995, *The Tonight Show* topped *Late Show with David Letterman* in the ratings for the first time, and won an Emmy for best variety show.

Jay's perseverance as *The Tonight Show* host even when the chips were down has made the show a huge hit and is now part of a famous show-biz success story.

they're very naive. They don't know much about life. You can't talk about sex, really, other than the thrill of it. So you can't share any of your life experiences."

When all else fails, trot out the condom-Geraldo joke.

"In New York City they're handing out condoms to high school students. Gee, I thought it was a big day when I got my class ring."

Or: "I hear there's talk of inaugurating a National Condom week. Now *there's* a parade you don't want to miss."

Or: *"Consumer Reports.* This month was their condom-testing issue. Spent the whole month testing condoms. Boy, I bet these guys couldn't *wait* to get to work in the morning."

Or: "I'll tell you something. I lost all respect for Charles Manson when he went on [Geraldo's] show."

Leno never had any pride when it came to using other people's jokes. He even stole them from his mother. When he told her he was having General Schwarzkopf as a guest, she said, "Oh, he's really good. I really liked him in those *Terminator* movies."

Another time, he told her Sylvester Stallone made $10 million for twelve weeks of work. "All she could say," cracked Leno, "was, 'Well, gee, what about the other forty weeks?' "

Leno had an even better joke about Stallone and Schwarzenegger. "Stallone and Schwarzenegger have opened up the acting profession to a lot of people who couldn't get into it when speech was a major requirement."

Leno finds it odd that "you can make fun of presidents and vice presidents but not sponsors. I mean it. I think the audience perceives advertising and corporations to be more powerful than the president or vice president." Maybe not so odd. Baiting sponsors is like biting the hand that feeds you.

Better stick to the political jokes. "Nancy Reagan's idea of the Third World is JCPenney."

Not that he has anything against Nancy Reagan or women in general. If anything, Leno is a feminist. "I always wondered who wrote the notes for the movies in *TV Guide*," he once mused. "And I realized it must be a man. It couldn't be a woman. I saw a listing: 'Nine o'clock—HBO movie. *Unmarried Woman*, the story of a divorced woman's struggle for respect and equality. Starring Alan Bates.'"

Hewing to a politically correct line, Leno generally tries to steer clear of jokes that offend women. And he never did like to do wife jokes.

"I mean, when you listen to comedy now, all marriages suck. Any woman you've been with more than a week is a bitch usually or bad sexually or something."

He believes that finding humor in abortion and women's rights is a taboo subject. He harbors no ambition to change the world and has no hidden agenda, because he is "not a social satirist. If it's funny, fine."

Leno is proud that nobody can determine his political affiliation. "I don't think anybody can figure out my politics. I'm not someone who hopefully ever will have his picture taken with a politician. If you get invited to the White House for something, that's different, that's a presidential thing. But if you're out there at a fund-raiser, you can't then go on *The Tonight Show* and make fun of the opposing candidate."

Anyway, to all intents and purposes, Leno was ready for whatever would happen by the time the 1990s rolled around. He had it made already. But there were plums he was willing to pick—if they came within reach. And suddenly they did come within reach—in fact, the most important one of them all did.

* * *

For the past seventeen years, Helen Gorman Kushnick had played a most important part in Jay Leno's professional life. He called her his manager, although she handled all sorts of jobs for him, including that of an agent as well. She booked him into gigs, she made his travel arrangements, she got him all different kinds of jobs. It was largely because of her hard-nosed professionalism that he was able to work in so many different places.

Helen had first seen Jay Leno at the Comedy Store in L.A. At the time, she was going out with Gerold Kushnick, a lawyer, and soon afterward, in 1979, she and Jerry married. They formed a management team—a company that concentrated on well-known comedians in the trade.

It was Helen who took over the management of Jay Leno's professional life and Jerry who took over the business end. Helen had a good instinct about Leno. She knew he would be big someday. She wanted to be with him to enjoy the rush of celebrity success when it came.

In 1980, Helen Kushnick had twins—Sara and Sam. They were born prematurely at Cedars-Sinai Medical Center and the two were given the usual blood transfusions as was the custom at that time with preemies.

When he was two and a half years old, Sam caught a bad cold that seemed never to go away. Physicians kept assuring Helen that the boy would recover, but he did not. One day he turned blue and she rushed him to Cedars. Nothing could be done for him. He lived only nineteen more days.

The reason he died was a hideous and horrid story. The blood that Sam had received by transfusion had been tainted with HIV virus, the virus responsible for AIDS—little known at that time.

Leno elaborated: "Sam was like the fourth child in Los Angeles to have AIDS. Or at least the fourth one that people knew about. It was like the flip side of winning the one-hundred-million-dollar California lottery, a one-in-a-million chance. It was a great tragedy."

Then, in 1989, six years after Sam died, Jerry Kushnick developed colon cancer and died. Two years later, Helen Kushnick underwent a mastectomy, with the breast cancer she suffered diagnosed as in remission.

It was on Jerry's deathbed that he extracted a promise from Jay Leno always to look out for his "two girls—Sara and Helen." And Leno promised.

The relationship between Helen and Jay Leno was a complex one. Jay Leno instinctively personified a "good guy"—"gentle Jay"—and knew it helped make him the personality he was. From his salesman father he had learned that the part he was playing as a comedian cast him as everybody's friend and made him well liked.

What Helen did was take over all the rough-and-tumble details of Jay's career. When the bookings got rough or the money wasn't right, it was Helen who argued and got the gigs changed or the numbers fixed. When mistakes were made it was Helen who caught the culprits and chewed them out. Because she was so persistent at her work it was a rare day that Jay Leno ever looked even the slightest bit bad.

Things went so smoothly with Helen around that Jay hardly noticed how aggressive and abrasive she could be. What was more, he was unaware of the glares of defiance sent in her direction by people close to him. He had become isolated and wrapped in cellophane by his eminence grise—a good thing for his jokes and his stage appearances, but not necessarily a good thing for his understanding of the nuances that made show biz the rough world it was.

Helen Gorman Kushnick, a New Yorker, was the daughter of an Irish truck driver and an Italian immigrant housewife. Not for nothing has the term *fighting* generally been closely aligned with the word *Irish*. She grew up in East Harlem. All her life she feasted on confrontation. It was her life's blood.

A close associate who had known her for years once explained what made her tick. "I call her a warrior, because she will just obsess on something and just push and push and push."

Better than endless confrontation, of course, was manipulation from a background position. And Helen, with all her in-your-face skills, was able as well to pull off a number of slick and subtle deals in a surreptitious manner.

Now she, who had spent all of seventeen years with Leno getting his bookings for him and wet-nursing him through all the details of his complicated and exhaustive day-to-day life, was, by 1991, beginning to get just a bit impatient. Time was slipping by. When Leno had been selected by Johnny Carson as *the* guest host for *The Tonight Show* in 1987, Helen had assumed that it would be only a matter of time before she would be able to collect her dues: *The Tonight Show* host job for Jay, and the executive producer job for her.

The point was: *When* was Carson going to give up the ship? Leno didn't really seem to care. He had a good berth there as guest host. He was making good money. Things had never looked better for him.

But what would happen to Leno when Carson quit? For years now David Letterman had been doing his job quietly in the 12:30

to 1:30 A.M. spot at NBC, following Carson. In the trade as well as in the public mind, Letterman had always appeared to be a kind of heir apparent to the throne that Carson had graced for so long. True, nothing had ever been said about Letterman's assumption to the throne, but the idea certainly existed in his mind, if in no one else's.

If Carson went, and Letterman filled his spot, what would happen to Jay Leno? The 12:30 to 1:30 spot? Or oblivion? Kushnick did not want to think about that.

And then quite abruptly, with no warning, the way seemed to open up for Helen Kushnick. She saw a stratagem by which she could bring about Johnny Carson's retirement—deviously, discreetly, on catlike paddy-paws—and bring on her own candidate for the plum job of night-time television.

The "other network" suddenly surfaced and began making certain overtures to her, and Helen knew that she had an answer of sorts for the molasses-in-January attitude of Johnny Carson toward his sign-off.

The "other network"—CBS—had been smarting for years because its late-night programming was running on empty. It had first aired five nights of one-hour action-suspense mysteries across the board at 11:30 P.M. CBS had then tried a late-night talk show comparable to *The Tonight Show* with Pat Sajack as host—but it had developed into an absolute disaster and had been pulled off the air in April 1990 after only fifteen months on the air.

Executives at CBS were aware of the fact that things seemed to be in a holding pattern at *Tonight,* with Carson simply going on and on. Wouldn't that make any up-and-coming star waiting in the wings a bit impatient? An impatient entertainer might be the answer for CBS. *Late Night with Jay Leno?*

An approach was made to Helen Kushnick. CBS might be interested in making a deal with Jay Leno if Leno was interested in changing his venue. The money CBS suggested looked mighty good. The deal involved moving the permanent guest host into the 11:30 spot at CBS and going mano a mano against Johnny Carson.

When Helen Kushnick told Jay Leno about her exploratory interview with CBS, he was only mildly interested. It was still his dream to do *The Tonight Show.* Nevertheless, Kushnick went to several more meetings with CBS execs and allowed the fact to leak out to some of the more astute NBC executives who might not be aware that Jay Leno was *liked* by *other* people *out there.*

And yet no move was made.

Inside, Helen Kushnick was beginning to smolder. Outside, something *seemed* about to happen. Yet when it did happen, it occurred in a spot some three thousand miles away from Burbank, where most of the smoldering was being generated.

On February 11, 1991, the *New York Post* printed a bold story with the headline: THERE GOES JOHNNY. The subhead below it read: NBC LOOKING TO DUMP CARSON FOR JAY LENO.

That laid it all on the line. And indeed no one in the television industry could say that the rumors had not been floating around for weeks and months already.

Bill Hoffmann and Timothy McDarrah were given credit for the story, which included a bunch of quotes from the "usual sources" speaking for "top honchos" at the NBC network. The gist of the statements was that the network wanted Carson "to sign off" so he could be replaced by Jay Leno. And the reason for the change—demographics. Jay Leno, the word went, "pulls in a younger audience more attractive to advertisers."

The NBC pooh-bahs were playing the nice guys, though. "Out of loyalty," the source went on to say, "they [the NBC heads] want to give him [Carson] one more year because it'll be his thirtieth anniversary on the air."

The story then meandered through the usual hills and dales of rumor and counterrumor, one the amusing thought that the NBC brass was far more concerned about who was going to tell Carson he was out than about any actual plans for the future. The story was written in such a fashion that it seemed to be moving in two different directions at once.

"Let the record show," said Curt Block at NBC, refuting the whole story as a vague, unconfirmed rumor, "that Johnny Carson will be the one who decides when he leaves the show." Another spokesperson pointed out that rumors had been circulating as long ago as fifteen years that Carson was through and was just waiting to hang up his spurs.

Buried in these innuendoes was the bare bones of an idea that the whole story was a very strong nudge to Carson, meaning explicitly that if he did not get the hint and begin to stir himself, the ax would soon be swinging down closer and closer to his neck.

Learning immediately of the headline and Block's rather empty words—to anyone but an idiot Block's statement was a thinly veiled vote of no confidence—Carson felt absolute humiliation. It sounded as though NBC was trying to eighty-six him instanter, the thankless so-and-sos. After all, he had only been with the ingrates for *thirty years.*

Jay Leno heard about it over the phone from a pal in New York. He knew that this might be a problem for him, but he shrugged it off; what was done was done. He simply thanked his caller and hung up.

But the network was infuriated. Quickly, a group of frustrated executives pounded out a rather meager story pledging great and unending support for and devotion to Johnny Carson. It was released to the press of the nation, a patently sorry effort by a network obviously flustered and upset at the ramifications of the leak.

Those close to Carson realized that the star felt absolutely devastated by the blow; he said little but was obviously morose. When he read the lap-dog promo piece that his bosses churned out at NBC, he was brought down even further. Most of those close to him thought Helen Kushnick was responsible for planting the story in the *New York Post*. This rumor finally found its way to Jay Leno.

Although he was not used to bracing her, Leno nerved himself up to track down Helen and check out the rumor. It was a simple question he then asked her. Did she have *anything* at all to do with this *New York Post* story?

Helen shook her head emphatically. She told him that the story did not emanate from her nor from anyone connected with her. She went on, speculating that it had actually come from the other side— that is, Carson's people—in a devious attempt to make it look a deliberate leak from Leno and company.

The idea, she went on, was to try to make Leno look bad, but the strategy had misfired and it was the Carson side that had suffered the most.

Leno got on the phone immediately to Carson. He told him that he and the people around him had had nothing to do with the *Post* story.

Carson's reaction was simple and effective. The story, he said, came from the Leno camp.

Leno repeated his statement that it had not and said how sorry he was that it had happened at all. And the conversation ended.

Carson was no fool. He could guess at the cutthroat infighting taking place behind his back to secure his coveted throne. Although Leno did not know it then, what added insult to injury in Carson's eyes was Leno's final denial that Kushnick had anything to do with the obviously planted disinformation.

In retaliation, Carson refused to invite Jay Leno to be his guest ever again, confining Leno's visits strictly to guest host jobs. Never again would Leno be able to sit across from Carson and chat in a friendly fashion. Leno survived the humiliation, and did not ponder it. It was Helen Kushnick who was irate at what Carson had done to her client.

For one thing, she knew it would make for a very uncomfortable changing of the guard at the show, if indeed Jay Leno *was* eventually selected to take over the spot. Helen felt that Johnny Carson should be welcoming Leno to the cherished position with open arms. Instead, Carson was ignoring Leno—making it look as if he didn't know he existed.

So enraged was Helen over Carson's cold-shouldering of her client that she was once heard to chant at one of Leno's staff meetings, when Leno wasn't present: "Die, Johnny Carson, die!"

The story in the *New York Post* was working to the advantage of Helen Kushnick, and, indirectly, to the advantage of Jay Leno, although he did not see it that way. In combination with CBS's earlier expressed interest in Jay Leno, the *Post* story formed two building blocks reaching up toward the coveted throne where Johnny Carson reigned.

It was time for Helen to move. Now that the forbidden words had been uttered—that Carson, God forbid, might retire!—she could go on to the next step. Who would fill his spot? She went to the two men under whose aegis *Tonight* operated: Warren Littlefield, president of NBC Entertainment, and John Agoglia, president of NBC Productions.

The gist of Helen Kushnick's pitch was the emptiness of the soon-to-be-vacated throne now occupied by Johnny Carson. There was also the frailty of Jay Leno's career at NBC. Helen pointed out that he could always explore the CBS offer in more detail. Or NBC might make him an offer to fill the spot when Carson moved on.

She reminded Littlefield and Agoglia that CBS had been buzzing around Jay Leno like bees around a flower garden—with very lucrative offers at that—to run a kind of rival *Tonight Show* on CBS.

As always, Jay Leno maintained a stolid silence in the face of money talk. He let Helen do all the work. There was no change in style here. He was pleased to be Mr. Good Guy, to let Helen do the bad-cop stuff to his good-cop image. And his manager did well by him, bringing up the danger of the CBS offer and hashing it through point by point.

It was time for action, Helen pointed out. Carson might even now be preparing to quit. If he did, a new host would be needed. Jay Leno was experienced; he was the heir apparent. Why not sign him up now, immediately, instead of going through protracted contract negotiations later on? The time to cut a deal was *now*, not later.

In the end, she got Littlefield and Agoglia to agree to sign on Jay Leno to take over the spot of host of *The Tonight Show*. The details of the contract were worked out on May 16, 1991, with the signing of the contract not to be a media event by any manner of means. While it was not necessarily secret, it was certainly a circumspect deal—not to be publicized in the media until Carson announced his own retirement.

The contract included the formal mechanism by which *The Tonight Show* would be turned over to Jay Leno as soon as Johnny Carson signed off on his last show. Jay Leno would succeed Johnny Carson at *Tonight*'s helm. In addition, Helen Kushnick would become executive producer of the show.

The deal stated that Jay Leno would be making about $3 million a year—a mere drop in the bucket compared to Johnny Carson's take. Kushnick's salary would be a large six-figure one. Once the details were all settled and the papers typed up that same afternoon, Jay Leno and Helen Kushnick affixed their signatures to the documents, and it was a done deal.

All in all, it was a contract that the two principals could be very happy about. And in addition it was a contract that the network could gloat over. NBC was indeed in the catbird seat.

Consider:

First, there would be no scramble now to find a star to fill Johnny Carson's shoes. Jay Leno had proved himself. The 11:35 spot would be filled then, adequately. And David Letterman's contract still had eighteen months to go for the 12:30 show he ran. With a lead-in by Jay Leno, and a finish with Letterman, NBC late-night had the best of all possible worlds.

For some reason, no one seemed to delve deeply into the situation with David Letterman and *his* feelings about the matter of Jay Leno and *The Tonight Show*. In fact, he had made 12:30 his own spot and thrived in it, making many millions as he toiled in late-night TV at the only network to stake out a solid position after midnight.

How would rumors of NBC's brand-new contract with Jay Leno play with David Letterman when he heard about it—as he was bound to do when Johnny Carson made his move to quit?

*   *   *

One week later, on May 23, 1991, Warren Littlefield was wrapping up his full roster of NBC stars to complete his huge talent presentation of the coming fall television schedule at New York's Carnegie Hall with a sure-fire surprise guest star—who turned out to be Johnny Carson, star of *The Tonight Show.* Carson had billed himself on the program a short time before it had commenced.

As Carson proceeded, the gags came sharp and fast. He even had a Carson special for Jay Leno. He said he had seen Jay earlier in the day and Jay was making a pest of himself worrying about Carson's health. When that laugh came on schedule, Carson delivered the capper, saying that Jay's idea of good health was for Carson to jog through Central Park about midnight that night.

Leno wasn't there in the audience. That busy man was on a plane flying back to Burbank.

And consequently he did not hear the message that Carson had taken such pains to insert in his presentation. He even hinted at it once in a rather discursive manner by pointing out that "as you well know," the year 1991 would be the last year Johnny Carson would be doing *The Tonight Show.*

If that wasn't enough, he waited until his conclusion to underline the point he had made earlier. Yes, he admitted with a smile as he closed out, his last show would be May 22, 1992—just about one year from that very day.

And that was it. It was an unanticipated bombshell in the middle of the network's routine presentation of its best entertainment features for the 1991 season. What he said was vitally important—but what he did not say was even more significant. He did not mention the name of any successor.

By the very starkness of the message, it became cataclysmically obvious that several very personal things had motivated Carson to deliver his message the way he had. He resented the story that everyone by now had decided was planted in the *New York Post* regarding his tenure at *The Tonight Show*. It had essentially forced him to state in public what his intentions were. He may have wanted simply to bide his time and make up his mind at his own pace. He was saying that he was pressured into quitting—and that rankled.

The NBC brass suddenly realized that it had hold of a hot potato—one that was burning their palms. Johnny Carson had announced his retirement. It was NBC's intention to announce that Jay Leno would be assuming the job as host for *The Tonight Show*. And—ye Gods!—what about David Letterman? *He* would have to be told all this immediately before it got to the public or it would be a public relations disaster. Now it was up to Littlefield and Agoglia to tell Letterman about Leno's snug little done deal.

Following the fall schedule presentation, rumors of all kinds began swirling through the halls of NBC once again. Some had it that Letterman would succeed Carson, as many people in the know had thought would be the case for some time. Others had it that indeed Jay Leno would be taking over. Leno heard the Letterman rumors. He knew the truth, of course. *He* would be taking over. His instinct was to shrug them off. And he did so. And yet there was always a chance. . . .

If Jay Leno had friends at the top at NBC, so did David Letterman. One of David's staunchest supporters was Peter Lassally, the producer of *The Tonight Show*. A cultured intellectual, born in Europe and a survivor of a German concentration camp, he had broken in on U.S. television by working for the *Arthur Godfrey Show*. He was admired for his sensitivity, his showmanship instincts, and his general savvy in the television world. The other supporter was Robert Morton, the producer of *Late Night with David Letterman*.

At the very first leak of the *New York Post* story back in February, Lassally had confronted Letterman and questioned him sharply about any understandings he might have had with top brass at NBC. There were none, Letterman replied. Lassally finally blurted out the question that had been bothering him and a number of other people at NBC.

"Don't you *want The Tonight Show?*"

Letterman said yes.

Lassally and Morton, the rumors went, prepared Letterman for the upcoming discussion with Littlefield and Agoglia. When the two executives ordered Letterman to the West Coast to discuss the matter, Letterman gave them back, issue for issue, a little comedic chortle of his own. He wasn't about to fly out to the West Coast to hear any bad news; they'd have to come to him.

And so Littlefield and Agoglia went to New York to meet with Letterman. The rumor mill ground out various versions of this story, but on one point there was definite agreement. At the end of the discussion, when Letterman was told that his contract forbade any jockeying about and that he would have to serve eighteen months more in the 12:30 to 1:30 slot, he uttered two sentences:

One. "Gentlemen, this is completely unacceptable."

Two. "I want you to release me from my contract."

And with that he stood up and walked out of the room.

Jay Leno, working harder than ever now, trying to prepare the best possible stand-up jokes he could for his regular appearances as guest host on *The Tonight Show,* decided to put all thoughts of the Letterman crisis out of his mind and concentrate on his work. And yet, in spite of the solid contract Helen Kushnick had hammered out for him and for her, and which was signed, sealed, and delivered, Leno knew how corporations worked. He could still be dumped.

The silence seemed to extend all around him. Nobody talked directly to him. Nobody wanted to bother him with such personal details. He kept wondering exactly what had gone down back in New York between Littlefield, Agoglia, and Letterman.

It took a long, haunted, gut-twisting two weeks for the news finally to seep out into the newspapers. The first story said it best:

Under a headline, "Carson Hands over Reins," the June 7, 1991, story went: "NBC made it official Thursday: Comedian Jay Leno will take over as host of *The Tonight Show* when Johnny Carson retires next year."

It added that Carson's last show would be May 22, 1992.

And the successor got to put in his two cents' worth: "Johnny's the best at what he does," Leno told *USA Today.* "I don't think we'll ever see the likes of it again. No one will ever hold an audience for thirty years the way Johnny has."

There was an added paragraph, somewhat jumbled, that quoted the New York *Daily News* saying, "David Letterman, the host of *Late Night with David Letterman,* who once was considered Carson's heir apparent, was described by an unnamed source as 'fit to be tied' when told of Leno's appointment."

That release did not sit too well with Jay Leno, who realized suddenly that he may not have understood all the ramifications of the discussions he had had with Littlefield and Agoglia.

Yet he was still "gentle Jay Leno" in his dealings with the press.

He never denied that he had politicked tirelessly for Carson's throne. As he continued to travel across the country on his road circuit, he continued to meet with NBC affiliates in different states, promoting himself. He wined and dined every executive who had time for him. He reminded them of his demographics on *The Tonight Show* and of his groundswell of popularity with the entire country, demonstrated by his three hundred or so successful gigs per year nationwide.

Leno put it this way:

"I've played every city in the country—including Alaska—at least once. I've worked with network affiliates, giving interviews, helping them do spots, selling tickets. I think I have them to thank." He meant thank for the job as host of *The Tonight Show.*

"And I take it as a compliment that people can't place me geographically."

He felt that his politicking helped him clinch the job. "I don't think I would have gotten this job if I'd gone through the normal testing and screening process."

Many observers had expected Letterman to get Carson's job. In the end, Letterman may have lost out because he didn't understand the behind-the-scenes political jockeying that always goes on in Hollywood. Leno not only understood it, he went out of his way to sell himself to every suit he met.

Leno claimed he never competed with Letterman for the job. "This is not a case of any sort of struggle going on. I've just been sitting in the wings, and when Johnny said he wanted to go, great. They called me, and I said, 'Yeah, fine, let's do it.' This isn't some sort of competition or power-struggle thing."

Leno went on, "I must admit I did not have a clue till it hit the papers that Dave had designs on the job."

According to many critics, that statement wasn't exactly the whole truth. They countered that Letterman had revealed in interviews published long ago that he had always wanted Carson's job.

Leno assured everyone that Letterman didn't have it in for him after Leno replaced Carson. If anything, it was just the opposite.

"Dave called me to congratulate me and stuff, and we're friends. And I think it's more the way it was handled. If two people live together and you tell your parents you're going to get married next Tuesday, that's not the same as saying you got married last Tuesday."

The *National Enquirer* said that Letterman "vowed to ruin" Leno's show in revenge.

Leno turned it into a joke. "Well, if there's anything Dave does, it's vow. When I speak to Dave, it's a word he often uses: 'I vow!' I can just *see* Letterman vowing."

Leno admitted that his and Letterman's friendship took a few knocks because Leno got Carson's show, but "it's not nearly as awkward as these things could be, were we not good friends. I sincerely think that if I didn't get the job, I would have wanted it to go to Dave, and I think he thinks the other way around.

"It's like two guys get in the ring, you know? You can be friends."

Johnny Carson later interviewed Letterman on his show to determine how Letterman really felt about the much-hyped coup by Leno.

Carson asked Letterman, "Just how pissed off are you?"

"You keep using language like that and you're going to find yourself out of a job."

"There were rumors you were going to bomb NBC."

Letterman had to snicker at that. "I hate waiting in line."

Carson finally got Letterman to answer seriously.

Letterman: "I'm not angry. I'm not angry at NBC about this. I'm not angry at Jay Leno about this. I'm not angry at you or the *Tonight Show* about this. Now if the network had come to me and said, 'Dave, we want you to have this show,' then a week later they said, 'Dave, we don't want you to have this show,' *then* I would have been angry. But I have a show and NBC can do whatever it wants to do with this show."

He added, "Now, would I *like* to have this show? Oh, sure— yeah."

It was said that when Letterman first heard the news that Leno had landed Carson's job, he was "fit to be tied." Letterman denied it, making a joke out of it. "I've never been tied in my life. There's not a man alive who can tie me!"

He went on, "I couldn't be happier. I think Jay'll do a fine job."

Carson said he had no idea why NBC chose Leno over Letterman. "NBC didn't ask me one way or the other. NBC never discussed it with me."

Leno made no secret of his exhilaration at replacing Carson. "This is the greatest thing that ever could happen. It's the same as an actor winning an Academy Award. It's the best job in show business."

Despite his politicking, Leno never really believed he would get the job because certain powerful showbiz figures told him he didn't have a snowball's chance in hell of supplanting Carson.

Leno elaborated. "This is a job I always wanted, that I always thought it would be neat to have. But I can remember casting people, people in television, saying to me, 'It will never go to someone who looks like you. Nor will it go to a Jewish guy. The show is too mainstream for that.' "

Carson never said so himself, but friends of his stated that he felt Letterman, not Leno, should have been offered his job.

Helen Kushnick believed it was her machinations that got Leno the prestigious job. She never mentioned the machinations—they were her secret—but she did talk to Leno familiarly.

"I've been serving you steak dinners for the last eighteen years. I just haven't bothered showing you how I slaughtered the cow."

Leno realized he must have been blind not to see how much Helen had been scheming for him. And, of course, for herself! But, why worry? He had the show!

Besides, it was too late to cry over past misdeeds. Jay Leno had a lot on his mind right then. He had to put his brand-new show together—and make it run.

The "New" Look

With a minefield of time bombs waiting to explode around him at any step he might take, Jay Leno decided to ignore all dangers and look only on the bright side. That meant that he intended to go on exactly the same way he had for so long already. From the beginning he did have several lucky breaks. There were influential people who did back up his selection as Carson's successor.

From the mainstream of comedy, columnist Art Buchwald said that he liked the idea of Leno replacing Carson. "He's a warm person," Buchwald said of Leno, "and it comes through in his humor. Johnny Carson is not a warm person." Buchwald also preferred Leno's political anecdotes to Carson's. "Leno is a lot sharper than Carson, particularly in his political humor."

For Buchwald, there was more to it than just the jokes. "For thirty years," he noted, "Johnny Carson has been the barometer for national humor. We all have to watch *The Tonight Show* to see what the American people are accepting. Now Jay Leno will be our national weatherman of humor."

Steve Allen called Jay Leno's appointment "delightful news." Coming from the first *Tonight Show* host, that was a good recommendation indeed for Jay and his fans. Allen certainly should know what he was talking about. "He's very good casting for the role," Allen said of Leno. "We're not guessing how he's going to do because he's done the show for several years, so there's no doubt about his qualifications."

Allen went on: "I would assume his chief popularity lies with the twenty-to-forty audience. But I'm in my sixties and I certainly enjoy his work." He then said, "I think he would have been just as successful twenty years earlier or twenty years into the future, for the simple reason that he is a likable, funny, witty fellow."

Jack Paar, another alumnus of *The Tonight Show,* had this to say: "I think it's fine. He'll do great. But Carson raised the monologue to an art. Carson can't be praised enough for what he's done for thirty years. I can't say that Leno will last thirty years. No one can touch Johnny. But I think people will come to love Jay as much as Johnny."

Mark Shields, a *Washington Post* columnist, agreed. "In 1988 [Leno] came close to Will Rogers. His monologues on politics are unequaled."

Warren Littlefield backed up the selection of Jay Leno to fill the to-be-vacated spot at *Tonight.* "Leno has proven extremely popular with the late-night audience and we are confident that the show will continue its late-night dominance for many, many years."

As for Jay Leno himself, he put the best possible face that he could on the situation. And made up jokes about the upcoming changeover. In one of his monologues he took a glance into the future, and came up with this: "Johnny's leaving, Ed's leaving, Doc's leaving. I feel like that kid from *Home Alone.*"

Never at a loss for japes and jests, he crafted another one-liner on the same subject. "This is probably the only job in the world where you get the job and they go, 'Okay, good! You'll be starting . . . in a year.' "

Leno had always had trouble believing that he would actually win the host spot at *The Tonight Show.* As late as 1991 when he was asked when he thought he would replace Carson he joked, "Roughly when Princess Margaret ascends the throne."

It was his opinion that "I kind of got *The Tonight Show* job the same way I've gotten everything else. I was never someone who anybody got particularly excited about. I mean, I've been with all the major talent agencies and been dropped by all of them."

None of the Hollywood types ever crowed about him, "Oh, you've got to see this kid, he's going to be the biggest thing ever!"

They would say stuff more like this: "You're not enough of this, you're not enough of that, you don't have a hook."

One reason Leno once gave for his success was his brief, child-like attention span. "The nice thing about doing *The Tonight Show* is that my attention span is about five minutes. And this is a show that is done in *real* time. There are no retakes. It's a lot like a nightclub. You walk in front of an audience, and you try out jokes. If they work, great. If they don't work, well, you try to do better tomorrow night."

He went further. "I also like the fact I can sit home and read the paper, look for material. Most comedians as soon as they think of something, they want to tell people. They want to go down to the club tonight. Now with *The Tonight Show* I can just go on TV and say it."

Leno admitted he had been lucky—even if his luck was an excruciatingly long time in coming. "I have been lucky in being able to build my reputation gradually through my stints as a guest host. I've been able to *sneak* in."

When asked if he should have a sidekick, he answered, "Pat Buttram comes to mind."

He was also asked if he should have guest hosts. "This is all so new that we haven't even thought about it. I don't want any other talk shows picking up on our ideas. I think that when I'm on vacation, we'll just do reruns. That'll amortize the product."

Of course he would have to cut back on his road shows. There simply wouldn't be time for them. "I'll continue to play clubs on the weekends while I host *The Tonight Show,* although I'll cut back on my travels somewhat. I've been on the road for twenty years. There's no place left to go!"

As Jay Leno faced mounting the throne to be vacated by Johnny Carson he was, as always, the eternal optimist. "I like to think people will tune in, even out of curiosity—like at a train wreck."

Leno loved everything about the show, even the interviews, which were actually the hardest things for him to do. In discussing the subject, he always overrode the difficulties he may have had by rationalizing a bit.

"Doing interviews is easy," he said. "These people are here because they want to be, plugging a book or a movie or something. This isn't an in-depth, secret probing of their lives. We're here to entertain and I try to keep the guest comfortable. It's not a problem at all."

And there was the fun he frequently had with the guests them-selves. "Guests I may not *personally* like usually turn out to be better than I expected. Even the worst people can *seem* very nice when they're all dressed up. And reasonably polite."

Because he is a thoroughgoing professional in all things comedic, Leno allowed himself to speculate a bit on the art of comedy and the way in which he approached it—Leno on Leno.

He had his own character and image well in hand. After mentioning that he had been wooed by other networks to do talk shows for them, he said that he had turned them down because he felt *The Tonight Show* was the greatest of all such shows. And that was the one he wanted to be associated with. Getting the show wasn't easy at all. In fact, it was fraught with uncertainties from the beginning.

"I've sort of been a good soldier," he said, not really doing the "aw, shucks" rube bit, but closing in on it. "The network gave me an indication that when Johnny was ready to retire, this would go into action. It was a preparation." They would say, "Can you do this?" to him. Why not? "I've worked Caesar's in Las Vegas since 1977. I've had the same manager for seventeen years. When I go somewhere, it's to stay. It's a bit like living together for five years and then deciding to get married. I like things that have a sense of history."

Leno turned philosophical. "There are two ways to get a major shot on TV. Either you stay in town and schmooze the casting directors and agents, so that you become well known in the industry, or you build a base around the country.

Leno on comedy:

"After you've been doing this for twenty years, you learn to go with your instincts. You know when you've done one Quayle joke too many. I meet *The Tonight Show* audience before the show. And don't forget, when you do a monologue every night, you feel an audience's reaction, pro or con. They give you a sense of what's appropriate and inappropriate. Johnny Carson can still read an audience better than anyone."

Getting *The Tonight Show,* Leno said, "is akin to being elected president. You're not playing a character. You get to be who you are. I'm exactly what people expect when they meet me. They don't say, 'You're not a doctor or a detective?' I don't have to learn scripts or spend all day on a movie set. You tell the jokes, do the monologue, it's all over and different the next day."

He added, "I *do* feel the responsibility. I've always led my life as though it was understood that I had to make moral decisions. I'll never show up drunk and embarrass *The Tonight Show.*"

The show itself, he said, was a part of a moral tradition. "When you think of some of the horrible things this country's been through—the assassination of John F. Kennedy and Martin Luther King, Jr., the Vietnam years—the fact that Johnny was able to get up night after night and find comedy in the day's events or find some way to make people laugh, that's a hard thing to do. Let *Nightline* handle the crises and Donahue ask the probing questions. On *Tonight* you want to have the lighter side. I hope it never changes."

Leno said, "I like to look back at the history of hosts and say, 'Gee, it's my turn not to drop the ball.' It's like being given the crown jewels. You hold on to them and make sure nobody steals them. Then you pass them on to somebody else."

*   *   *

The media was abuzz with the contretemps stirring just below the surface at NBC. Rick Du Brow, in the *Los Angeles Times,* described what he considered to be NBC's "bungling" of *The Tonight Show* negotiations. "Here, on the one hand, was Letterman, the most dominant TV entertainment figure in the 1980s, the person who changed the medium by bringing to it the view of the TV generation—and the host of a financial and ratings success.

"And there, on the other hand, was Leno, a superb wit about current events and a highly agreeable fellow, who NBC came to believe was the choice because he also was successful and was regarded by many as very mainstream, in the tradition of Carson."

However, by the many accounts of observers involved in the negotiations for a successor to Carson, "NBC management simply handled the situation very badly, giving rise to fast-spreading reports that Letterman was 'furious,' and might even be considering trying to break his network contract" (which indeed he was).

A source close to *The Tonight Show* said that NBC "completely misjudged" Letterman in its negotiations for a successor. "They bumbled. He's in a great position to ask for the moon." Another source said, "I think NBC screwed up. I don't know what took so long to set this up. This job was going to Jay for the last year or so. The deal's been set for a couple of weeks."

And, screwed up and bungled though the situation with David Letterman might be, it was certainly clear-cut and precise to Jay Leno and Helen Kushnick. There was just about a year to go before Jay would be sitting at *The Tonight Show* desk. During that almost-year, the two of them would be honing things to perfection so the debut would be something no one would forget.

* * *

For the balance of 1991, Jay Leno continued his guest host jobs on *Tonight* just as he had been doing since 1987. And although Helen Kushnick would not take over as executive producer until May 1992, she had actually been putting in her two cents' worth in regard to almost everything about the show since as far back as 1987. A "source" at *Tonight* told *Entertainment Weekly* that she "was always butting in, especially in booking guests."

The "butting in" did not involve any of the writing chores. The two separate staffs (in Leno's case *he* was the staff) kept to themselves. "We never used Johnny's writers," Kushnick said. "Jay came in as a self-contained unit."

The rumblings that began in 1987 now continued at a higher decibel rate, although there was no open feud—yet. After all, Carson might have been on his way out, but his continued *Tonight Show* appearances were models of grace, comic genius, and superb theatrics.

And everybody knew who the king *was*. There were no mistakes about that. But the reverberations of discontent were even then beginning to cause slight ripples to fan out on the usually placid outer surface of *The Tonight Show*.

Certainly NBC was not resting on its laurels and waiting for assistance from Jay Leno to publicize the coming change of stars on *The Tonight Show*. Early in January a cryptic story appeared in *Crain's* to the effect that Jay Leno had been named permanent host of *The Tonight Show* on May 25, 1991, almost a year ago, and that he would be taking over on that date in 1992. In effect, the piece was nothing more than a memory jogger designed to keep his name in front of the public.

Actually, the story was the first in a series of publicity shots that covered the whole range of *Tonight* activities. The idea was to build slowly to a shrieking crescendo in April and May to push the show higher in the ratings numbers.

In January *Broadcasting* published an insightful and punchy puff piece on Edd Hall, the announcer who had been hired to replace Johnny Carson's Ed McMahon. The Edd Hall piece managed to feature Jay Leno rather than Edd Hall, but no one seemed to mind.

In February *People* magazine ran an excerpt from a small book by Nancy Cobb titled *How They Met.* This was a collection of romantic encounters of people in the public eye—true stories of how famous couples met and wooed and married. Although Mavis Leno, formerly Nicholson, was the featured player in the anecdotal story, Jay Leno still managed to be the anchor of the whole piece.

In March Jay Leno was featured on the cover of *Time* magazine, with an adulatory story about his character and image as the Mr. Nice Guy of Show Business, along with felicitous details of his comedic style. The long piece ran parallel to a nostalgic and sincere tribute to Johnny Carson and his amazing thirty years as the king of late-night television.

In April Arsenio Hall managed to get in a couple of nasty swipes at Jay Leno in a story in *Entertainment Weekly.* The two entertainers would be going head to head against each other later in the year—only in certain cities, of course—and apparently Hall wanted first crack at Leno. The attack was personal and at the same time oddly oblique. Hall was apparently disturbed by Jay Leno's constant references to his "friendship" with Arsenio Hall.

The piece contained a quotation by Hall about their actual association with one another. "I always hear that Jay and I are friends when they interview him," he said. "I have no problem about saying good things about my competitors, but Jay Leno and I aren't friends! And you know what? *I* wasn't anointed, O.K.? No one put the late-night silver spoon in *my* mouth. I earned every drop of *mine*. . . . And I'm gonna treat him like we treated the kid on the high-school basketball team who was the coach's son. . . . We tried to *kick his ass,* and that's what I'm going to do—kick Jay's ass."

Putting on a face of bewilderment for the public, Leno wondered aloud at Arsenio Hall's diatribe against him. He had associated with Hall during his early days in Hollywood. The two had written jokes together. Leno had invited Arsenio and his mother to his house. He considered it a good-natured friendship. That Hall was considering it nothing more than a professional association of rival celebrities was all right with Jay Leno; if Hall wanted it to appear that they weren't friends, so be it.

It was obvious that Arsenio Hall sensed what was in store for the future. *Tonight* would try to chase Hall's show off the air. Jay Leno was an insatiable competitor, even with that nice-guy front. Hall was getting in his licks early on. And bookings were the name of the game at that 11:30 hour. It was *who* you got, not *how* you treated them when they were on.

It is a distinct possibility that Arsenio Hall had already felt the sharp sting of Helen Kushnick's aggressiveness in booking stars. But that was all speculation at the time, and would have to be studied as the situation progressed.

In April, Digby Diehl ran a story in *TV Guide* titled "Jay Leno: Is He Up to It?" Diehl had sensed a deliberate smoothing over of Jay Leno's cutting edge in his recent political and sociological material. He seemed prepared to become nothing more than another comic getting off on the usual comedy-club routines. There was a hint that by the time Leno took over, he would have lost all the razor-sharp edge that had made him what he was when he first came on the scene.

In May the *New York Post* ran a story about the graphics company that put together the opener that would be used to introduce Jay Leno to his audience every night. While the story played up the details of the opener, which had the camera swishing through dozens and dozens of different colored and textured curtains—purportedly representing Leno's appearances on hundreds of stages throughout the country—the article had a rather sarcastic tenor to it.

But the print media faded almost into nonexistence as the *days* grew short before Leno's debut—and the electronic media suddenly took over.

In March, Jay Leno was interviewed by Steve Kroft on *Sixty Minutes*. In May, Jay Leno visited Oprah Winfrey in Chicago, talking to her for the full hour of the show. One day later, Leno was talking to Barbara Walters on her ABC-TV show. The Walters segment featured both Johnny Carson *and* Jay Leno. "Johnny and Jay are Hollywood institutions with mainstream tastes," she said, setting the tone for the spot.

Nine days later Jay Leno was on *Later with Bob Costas,* which aired at 1:30 A.M. following the David Letterman show. This was a two-hour jaunt through Jay Leno's life. But the main target was the upcoming show, and Leno was voluble about his new music director, Branford Marsalis.

"What do you think's the key to staying power and what's the definition of staying power?" Costas asked Leno at one point.

"Oysters," Leno shot back.

On May 25, Leno was interviewed by Katie Couric on *The Today Show*. If anything, it showed what an indefatigable worker Jay Leno was. He would be opening his new show that same night!

Johnny Carson's final show the previous Friday night had been a blockbuster. It was exactly the kind of heartwarming thing that everybody expected and wanted. By the time it was over, there wasn't a dry eye in the house.

Jay Leno watched carefully. It was a great show—the kind of thing he dreamed about doing some day himself. However, he noted that one thing was missing. There was no mention of who would be filling the spot managed so dramatically and wonderfully by Johnny Carson.

It was as if Jay Leno did not exist.

For the opener of Jay Leno's *Tonight Show,* Helen Kushnick had signed on Billy Crystal, a pal of Jay Leno from the old days, and a recent smash hit as emcee of the Academy Awards in Hollywood. She balanced Crystal up with a somewhat oddball guest. His name was Robert Krulwich, CBS's satirical television observer of the economics scene. Satire on economics could be devastatingly funny. Robert Benchley's two-reeler on the corporate financial report was a classic example. However, satire was a tricky business, and if it misfired it could bury the show.

The stand-up had been honed and shaped over agonizing days and nights until it was just right. Jay Leno felt it was the best he could do.

During the day of May 25, Jay seemed the coolest of all the members of the *Tonight* staff. He was upbeat, helpful, smiling. Maybe even just a bit bored by it all.

A couple of hours before the show aired, Bob Wright, the president of NBC, called Helen Kushnick in her office. Wright was a curious composite of a high-up General Electric executive and a somewhat savvy television exec. He had assumed control of the network when he came in with a number of other G.E. executives after NBC's purchase by G.E.

Wright was telephoning from his Connecticut home. He came right to the point. He asked Helen exactly how *The Tonight Show* was going to open.

Helen Kushnick told the president of NBC that the show would begin with Jay Leno's usual monologue.

Wright actually wanted more information than that: He wanted to be sure that Jay Leno was going to open the show ith a nice thank you to his predecessor, Johnny Carson.

Now Kushnick was abrupt, telling Wright that they were not going to do anything special about thanking Carson.

Wright, taken aback, wanted to know why not.

Kushnick did not give the obvious answer—that is, that Johnny Carson had not once mentioned the fact that his successor was going to be Jay Leno. What she did say was that they didn't want the new show to have any ties to the past.

Wright was not impressed. He told her quite simply that she was making a terrible mistake, and again urged her to tell Jay to acknowledge his predecessor. Helen told Wright that she could not ask Jay to do that. And that was the end of the conversation.

As for Jay Leno—Mr. Good Guy, the "gentle one," Mr. Nicey-Nicey—thanking Johnny Carson was certainly at the top of his list of things to do on opening night. He had not mentioned it to Helen Kushnick at all, but after her chat with Bob Wright, she thought that she should give him her thoughts on the subject.

And when she mentioned the subject to Jay, it was with a firm shake of the head.

Grimly, Leno disagreed, but not out loud. After all, he owed almost everything he had won in getting *The Tonight Show* to Helen Kushnick *as well as* Johnny Carson. How could he go against her wishes? She was his manager. She was his boss, in a way, too. There was a delicate, somewhat fragile, arrangement there.

In most cases, it would have been a simple matter. He would have said thanks anyway and then settled the obvious discontent later on as best he could.

But Leno had left himself so much in the hands of Helen Kushnick that he could not think of going against her. He agonized over the problem, knowing how steely hard his manager and executive producer was. He had weathered her temper tantrums before. So had everyone else on the show.

"In my mind," he told a magazine writer later, "if I had said something about Johnny on live TV, I thought she would have gone nuts and started screaming at me on the air. I thought, Oh, Jeez, let me just get through this. But I didn't enjoy it. After that show, I didn't say, 'Hey, let's have a party!' I remember saying to myself, 'Why aren't I enjoying this? Why isn't this fun? Why don't I care anymore?' And I thought, Is this what it's going to be for the next twenty years?"

At the time he chickened out and decided to abide by Helen Kushnick's rules. However, he did manage to discuss the problem with the person who was the closest to him of anyone in a personal sense. His wife, Mavis, urged him to go against Helen's wishes. Nor was Mavis alone in her advice to him. All of Leno's staff agreed with her.

But Leno was a good soldier, and he obeyed the boss. To his later regret and to his universal discredit, actually. In the act, he did come off looking like some kind of uppity ingrate—and not a faithful follower of a much-loved role model.

*   *   *

The new show started out pretty much the way everybody thought it would. Jay's stand-up was polished and delivered boffo so that everyone could laugh at the jokes as they came up.

There was, of course, an obligatory Dan Quayle joke. *"The Tonight Show,"* Jay Leno said, is the show that the vice president "hates even more than *Murphy Brown.*"

That was followed by the obligatory Murphy Brown joke. "One thing you can say about Murphy Brown that you can't say about Dan Quayle—she'll be back in the fall."

And that, of course, was followed by the obligatory Ross Perot joke. "The less he says the more popular he gets." Pause. "Which is something that Dan Quayle has yet to grasp."

The Dan Quayle Obligatory Joke IV: "Where would I be without my father?" Leno had Quayle wondering in a Jay Leno one-liner. "Probably in Vietnam."

Plus a Bill Clinton bonus gag thrown in. "Sex is a deeply personal matter, Bill Clinton insists—between a candidate and his campaign volunteers."

At the beginning of the routine there was an obligatory Jay Leno joke inserted to remind people of what they were seeing that night: "Let's see how you all feel in thirty years," Leno quipped.

When Billy Crystal came on, he had a song he had parodied for the show. To the tune of "You Made Me Love You," he sang his own inspired lyrics and wound up with the familiar double refrain about not wanting to fall in love at all. And so on. Good for a few laughs.

Then Crystal did an Ed McMahon joke, relating that he had seen the ex-announcer of the show standing out in the parking lot carrying a sign that read: "Will announce for food."

At the end of Crystal's stint, Shanice, a pop singer, sang two numbers. She was followed by Robert Krulwich, CBS's economics correspondent. He attempted a parody lecture on how corporate CEOs are paid too much.

At one point Krulwich said, "Knowing that the budget for this show isn't quite what it was four days ago—" He meant when Carson was running things.

Leno nodded. "Yeah, it would be a shame if we couldn't put guests up in a hotel."

"CBS paid for my flight out here," Krulwich said, hinting at NBC's tight-fisted expenses policy.

"They're going to have to pay for the flight back, too," Leno said with a smile.

The critics were uniformly displeased with the debut. "Jay's first night was almost as sad as Johnny's last night," Tom Shales wrote in the *Washington Post*. Then he zeroed in on what he considered a major gaffe.

"The most shocking thing was . . . the fact that Leno never once stopped the show to pay a moment's serious tribute to Carson, the much-adored icon whose chair he aspires to fill and who first hired him to be guest host five years ago."

Shales didn't particularly like the show itself, except for a few individual elements that drew his mixed reactions. Overall, he wrote, "Everything seemed scaled back and smaller somehow, including the personality of the man in the host position. One of Leno's bad habits is laughing at his own jokes, sometimes with a tee-hee giggle. He makes spitting sounds during some punch lines. His in-your-face face could be a problem over the long haul, too. Even the short haul."

John J. O'Connor of *The New York Times* praised the addition of Branford Marsalis as musical director of *The Tonight Show*. "Decidedly on the plus side for Mr. Leno," he wrote, "is the recruitment of Branford Marsalis . . . overseeing a house band culled from his own group of jazz musicians. Obviously rattled by some of the pre-opening publicity given to Mr. Marsalis, Mr. Carson went out of his way in the final shows to heap praise on Doc Severinsen and the band."

O'Connor also pointed out Jay Leno's oversight in not thanking Johnny Carson in his opening remarks, saying that although Billy Crystal's "song," reminiscent of Bette Midler's song to Johnny Carson the week before, gave Leno an "opportunity to be more gracious than his predecessor, who had failed to even mention him," Leno had fumbled the occasion away.

Diane Werts of *Newsday* thought Leno's opening show was a "tense performance," analyzing it from a merchandising standpoint. "Leno seemed to be walking a tightrope of expectations, wanting not to scare away Carson's fans while still establishing his own *Tonight Show* tone. In his guest-host appearances over the years, he's done that simply by being himself—younger, sharper, looser, wilder; more in touch with new music, hip references, and cooler kinds of humor. But now that the gig's his, he appeared almost to retrench in terms of attitude, letting the look of the show make the statement instead."

"Leno, now that he's the leading man rather than the stand-in, is much more manic than Carson," according to Ed Siegel of the *Boston Globe*. "Everything from his giggle to his head-bobbing to his delivery seemed overexcited."

Daily Variety's Van Gordon Sauter gave a more positive review than his fellow newspaper critics. "Leno is a smart trouper who knows his medium and his audience. Even with the fragmentation of the time period and the talk genre, one suspects he will assemble a commercially credible audience and achieve longevity—which for television . . . is anything that lasts longer than Prince Andrew and Fergie."

Rick Du Brow of the *Los Angeles Times* concluded that, "In the end, though, the future of *The Tonight Show* under Leno will probably be determined by how well his staff provides the comedian with guests who dovetail with his personality and enable him to sharpen his interviewing—and thus finish strong in the final forty-five minutes of his nightly series."

Even so, the harm was done in the negative reviews that pointed out the nonworking elements of the show, including Jay Leno's obvious snubbing of Johnny Carson, his mentor. However, Helen Kushnick reveled in the fact that Carson had not been mentioned once in the new show. At the end of the broadcast she was so elated she could not contain herself and yelped out loud in the middle of the set:

"Fuck you, Johnny Carson!"

The Bookings War

The snubbing of Johnny Carson on Jay Leno's first night as *The Tonight Show* host was a shocker that was not easily passed over by people who knew Jay Leno. What had happened to gentle Jay? Where had his decency gone? What had happened to his sense of propriety?

Most accepted it immediately as a high-hat attitude that was strange to him, but that apparently came with the new territory he had coveted, wooed, and won. Whether or not the fight in getting that territory was fair or unfair made no difference. He had shown the world—and especially the tight little world of show biz—exactly where he now stood.

Overnight, longtime friends in the comedy business threw up an invisible wall against him, creating a zone of silence around him—in effect, deserting him. After all, he had become a danger to their careers, thanks to his first-night attitude toward his predecessor.

Appalled at Leno's tactlessness, nighttime talk-show hosts Arsenio Hall and Dennis Miller both hastily put the kibosh on their friendship with him. Of course, Arsenio Hall had already begun to circle the wagons against him in his earlier *Entertainment Weekly* manifesto. Dennis Miller was another case of an early friend who was no longer a friend.

Overnight, Leno became something of a pariah in the comedy world, and he professed to those around him that he could not understand why. What had he done that was so despicable? He had obeyed his boss. That was part of the game. What was so wrong with that?

To find out why everyone had suddenly begun to treat him like the plague, he sat down to talk to Helen Kushnick. If anyone should know, Leno thought, she should. It was her business as his manager and agent to know these things.

She knew very well why he had become a pariah. She had caused it to happen by her own deep-seated personal grudge against Johnny Carson. As Leno waited there for some kind of an answer to his heart-to-heart with her, she realized she could not tell him the truth at all. If he hadn't the sense to figure out what had gone wrong, he was too dense to tell straight on. Instead she went into one of her usual tirades.

"Go write your fucking jokes!" she shrieked at him, waving her arms and pushing papers around. "I'll handle the business!"

About this time the *New York Post* ran a follow-up story to its earlier February blockbuster scoop about NBC, Carson, and Leno. The story maintained that NBC had actually wanted Carson to resign *before* May 22, but had decided that any time would do on a better-late-than-never basis. In fact, the piece had Helen Kush-nick's fingerprints all over it, and it is surprising that Leno did not immediately catch on.

But then, he had believed her when she told him previously that she had nothing to do with planting the first So Long, Johnny Carson story. And so now, with *The Tonight Show* firmly in her grasp as executive producer, she began to initiate some of her own special rules and regulations that in turn began to affect the bookings on *The Tonight Show.*

What later became the Bookings War affected not only the bookings at NBC but the bookings, in particular, of Arsenio Hall's syndicated show at Paramount. It later came out that it was Hall that Kushnick wanted to go head to head with. It was the fresh-ness and the hipness of the show that was bringing in a younger late-night audience—and the younger audience was crucial to the success of Jay Leno's new *Tonight Show* too.

Luckily, it had been Arsenio Hall who *started* the rather theat-rical feud when he vowed to bust Leno's ass. At least no one could blame Leno for starting the fight.

Up to the night that Johnny Carson presented his last *Tonight Show*, Helen Kushnick did not turn her hand fully to the nitty-gritty of booking the guests. But once Leno was installed, she knew she had free rein to do whatever she wished. And so a new, hardened competition for big and influential names became evident in the world of late-night television.

In what now appeared to be "the good old days," there had been some give and take among talk-show hosts and the guest book-ings. *The Tonight Show* one night, perhaps Arsenio Hall's show the following week. Perhaps even sooner. There were no real rules laid down. The new hard line began to solidify without anyone paying much attention to it. The public simply did not care to know about the details. And the ones in the know confined themselves to rumors and whispers.

One early skirmish in the bookings battle concerned a booking of Elizabeth Taylor on the Arsenio Hall show. Kushnick took umbrage at the fact that the appearance was to support an AIDS foundation that Taylor was running. Helen Kushnick had her own interest in AIDS, and in turn thought the two women should support each other. She asked the actress to cancel her Arsenio booking and appear on *Tonight.*

The actress was a foot soldier in many a war of gigantic egos, and she refused point-blank to take on Kushnick. And so the matter ended—for a while. Helen resumed the confrontation, putting pressure on Taylor. How about the legal details of her AIDS foundation? Were there any details she had slipped up on? Was it properly registered? And so on.

Of course, all this byplay was grist for the rumor mills, and soon the entertainment world was reverberating with charge after charge. Even if the details were obscured, it was obvious that there was some kind of bad blood operating between the two women. Taylor's attorney wrote a letter to Kushnick demanding that she quit any such inquiries into Taylor's AIDS foundation.

Things simmered on the back burner for a bit, and soon enough the whole thing blew over. Taylor appeared on Arsenio. However, there were aftershocks. A circus act called the Cirque du Soleil had appeared at a benefit produced by Elizabeth Taylor. Quite suddenly the Cirque du Soleil was *unscheduled* from *Tonight*'s lineup. In mock innocence, Helen Kushnick noted that the Cirque had appeared several times before on *The Tonight Show*. So what was the big deal?

Actually, in view of the ratings Jay Leno was getting, there was no reason there should be any kind of quarrel between the two shows at all. In June, just after he debuted as host of *The Tonight Show*, Leno was running a strong 5.2 rating, which held up through June. The 5.2 rating, incidentally, was the same rating that Johnny Carson got exactly one year before he quit the show. By November, *Tonight* was averaging 4.6 a week. Opposite him in November, Arsenio Hall was going along at about 2.7 or so. However, Hall was down about 20 percent from his ratings two years prior to that point.

Oddly enough, in the ratings battle, the winner of the total event for 1992 seemed to be a show that had nothing to do with the talk-show format. It was Ted Koppel's politically oriented *Nightline*. It was garnering a 4 rating in June, but by November, it had risen to a 5 average! Certainly the presidential election helped.

Despite *Nightline*, Leno was elated at the numbers. "Any time you can hold your own, that's great," he said. "When you look at the late-night market, especially this year . . . you can hold your own, that's something to be proud of."

Helen's maneuverings looked very much like unfair booking practices to many in the industry. Keeping a person off a competing show after appearing on *Tonight* or off *Tonight* if he or she had appeared recently on another show was a classic example of extortion—or at least it *amounted* to extortion in the long run.

Agents were complaining bitterly to NBC about her, and some of the executives mentioned these practices to Leno, but he did nothing about Helen, claiming that he did not know what was going on but that he thought everything was working out well *in the ratings*. So?

Leno finally talked to Helen, but she blamed the contretemps on the fact that she was a woman and the Hollywood game was a man's game. Later, she told Phil Donahue: "It's always the same story. Every time a woman gets into a position of some kind of authority where they're not wanted, they're considered crazy, hysterical, a nut."

And Helen's aggressiveness in other instances riled many an influential Hollywood potentate. They did not like the way she ensured network loyalty by forcing NBC personality Maria Shriver to break her promise to guest on *The Tonight Show*'s rival, *Arsenio*.

"Am I competitive?" asked Helen about this specific booking. "Sure. But the rules were set before us. Getting people first is the name of the game."

Critics found her hardball tactics crude, to say the least.

Nevertheless, Helen Kushnick was not about to declare a truce in her battle with Arsenio Hall's show. Instead, she worked out her own private policy of booking on *The Tonight Show*. A *Tonight* staff member was quoted by Peter J. Boyer in a *New Yorker* piece: "Her policy was: Every record company, every movie company, every publicist is going to have to choose from now on—either they do us or they do Arsenio." Basically, the policy demanded that guests appear first on *Tonight* and then only on *Tonight* in perpetuity.

It was bound to happen—and it did. Travis Tritt, a country singer who had been on *Tonight*, broke the unwritten rule that Kushnick had dreamed up and was booked for *Arsenio*. When Helen Kushnick found out about it, she telephoned Tritt's manager, Ken Kragen, to tell him that if Tritt actually showed up on the Hall show, he would never again be on *Tonight*.

Kragen tried to be conciliatory. "I feel badly about this. But I can't walk away from an obligation I made on another show."

Kushnick listened without a word.

"I could give him to you a week later," Kragen went on, "or I could give him to you in January when [his] CBS movie comes out, and maybe add some other elements—such as Kenny Rogers."

Kushnick's response was cold. "We don't do theme shows."

The conversation went nowhere.

Tritt appeared on *The Arsenio Hall Show*.

Kushnick was on the phone to Kragen the next day. After some sparring about, the basic message from Helen Kushnick was this: "Look, it's real simple. Travis Tritt is never going to do this show again. You and I are going to see each other around town; we're never going to talk again. It's your loss, you and the record company." And that was that.

Quite suddenly and unexpectedly, Kragen learned that there was a lot more to it than a simple blackballing of Tritt. Trisha Yearwood, another of Kragen's performers, was suddenly yanked from *The Tonight Show* lineup. It was obvious to Kragen that this was a deliberate move on Helen Kushnick's part to punish Kragen and his stable of singers for breaking *The Tonight Show*'s rules.

Kragen had fighting smarts too, just like Helen Kushnick. He knew what to do in this case. He telephoned the *Los Angeles Times*. Kragen gave his story of the bookings scrap to Daniel Cerone.

In the story, Cerone quoted Kragen as saying: "You try to stay out of those conflicts, where people are bitter rivals or competitors. But sometimes you're drawn into it. What you don't expect is people involved are going to then take it out in a way that's vindictive, when all you're trying to do is be honest and straightforward."

Kragen went on in the *Times*: "The last thing I ever want— and I can't tell you how many times I've bitten my tongue in this business—is to have a war with anyone. I think they're wasteful. But one thing has triggered my willingness to talk about this. That was when [Kushnick] vindictively took Trisha Yearwood off the show because of her dispute with me about being unable to book Travis Tritt on the show. That was my flashpoint, the point at which I have to say, Now this woman is injuring one of my clients who is an innocent bystander in order to try and get back at me in any way she can, because I didn't cave in to her threats."

Obviously, the *Los Angeles Times* story settled nothing. If anything, it only stirred the coals almost into flame. The rumors had been flying about for three or four months—ever since Jay Leno had ascended the throne of late-night television. And now here were indications that the rumors were true.

The problem was a crucial one. To all outward appearances, *The Tonight Show* in its new form had come on strong with a solid response of approval not only from the top brass, but from the public as well. And now, with the Summer Olympics taking a chunk out of Jay Leno's time on camera, and the presidential election beginning to edge out almost anyone who tried to make a point anywhere, the trouble brewing inside the show threatened to burst and consume the entire enterprise.

The *Times* piece was the catalyst. The top NBC brass huddled quickly and decisively. Helen wasn't just buffaloing talent agents. She was pushing around network and staff execs too. In short, Helen was alienating just about everyone she met. There were many examples of screaming tantrums on the set and in her office—blowups that made her look as if she were teetering on the edge of hysteria. It was time to lay down the law.

Warren Littlefield had warned Helen on many occasions that she was venturing beyond the pale with her sandbagging booking practices. She took little heed of his admonitions. On September 17, 1992, he had had a stomachful of her. She had been executive producer of *Tonight* for only four months—but she was out of control.

He phoned her while she was home in the silk-stocking Hidden Hills neighborhood in the San Fernando Valley where she lived in a palatial ranch house. He told her in no uncertain terms to shape up or ship out—that is, cut out the unfair booking practices.

Helen objected. Helen refused. Helen would not change her methods. After all, they were working! Look at the ratings!

The next day, September 18, she met with Leno and Littlefield. The three of them had a heated discussion, with Leno still supporting Kushnick, and afterward Helen called a meeting of her staffers to chew *them* out. She singled out a producer named Bill Royce for abuse, berating him for booking the wrong guests. She slammed him for belonging to a "cabal" that was out to get her.

Fed up with her bellyaching, Royce resigned in protest. He would later be rehired.

Meanwhile the brass were huddling as well. It was decided on the spot: Kushnick had to go. The question that immediately arose was an urgent one. Would Jay Leno go with her? In no way could Jay Leno be written off as a hothead, but a man did have his pride. He had been a willing dupe of Helen Kushnick's manipulations all his years in show business. Why should he change now?

If he did go, it would be a public relations disaster. He would go to CBS, of course, a network that had already put out friendly feelers for him. And if he went, he would be a formidable competitor to whoever would next sit behind the vacated desk at *The Tonight Show*.

On the night of September 20, 1992—a Sunday night—Warren Littlefield and John Agoglia called on Jay Leno at his home. It was not the first time they had discussed this problem. They had met twice on the Friday before, trying to hash out some kind of working arrangement to survive the crisis.

Once Jay Leno had said: "The show's doing okay, right?"

"It's doing well. Not spectacular, but well." However, Littlefield went on, "the town is going to rise up and choke you. They are rooting for you to fail, because of the hatred. It's not just competitive—it's their hatred for Helen Kushnick."

Leno got down to the nitty-gritty in one exchange with Littlefield. What would happen, he asked Littlefield, if Jay Leno walked out with Helen Kushnick?

Littlefield had already worked out his stand on that point. He said that he hoped Leno would stay with the network, but that if he did go, NBC would replace him with David Letterman.

And that was the way things were when Leno was visited by his two bosses Sunday night. Since all the points had already been taken up, this was simply a rehash of the arguments leading up to the final decision.

In careful tones, but in precise diction, the two men explained that Helen Kushnick was totally out of control. She had created a monster when she had laid down rules of exclusivity in booking guests for *The Tonight Show*. She had alienated numbers of people in the business. What she had been doing was now, of course, a matter of public knowledge. The public knowledge could only hurt *The Tonight Show*—which up to that point had been doing relatively well in the public's view.

Littlefield and Agoglia told Jay that they had all thought it through. Helen Kushnick *had* to go. There was no question about it. She was *out* as of this moment. There was only one question that remained to be answered.

Long ago in his career in show business he had made a decision regarding Helen Kushnick. She was there to do his bookings, get him where he was supposed to be, take care of his contracts, and so on. For that reason, he had given up a great deal of his independence, and thrust it onto her. He understood that.

But there was loyalty to be considered. She had been his only manager-agent for seventeen years. And she had brought him to the top of the profession. She had gotten him exactly what he wanted—what he needed to survive as Jay Leno.

He was torn in two directions. It was a terribly painful ordeal for him to go through. After Littlefield and Agoglia left, he went back to the phone. He called Helen Kushnick again, and talked to her. Then he called other associates. He was back to Helen some time later.

In one of the exchanges Helen tried to apply the supreme pressure on Jay Leno. She had put everything on the line for him, she said. She had done it all to help him. Yes, and that had included planting that *New York Post* story for him—to get Johnny Carson to make his move. Without that deed done, Jay Leno would still be doing guest host shots every week.

Leno's mood turned sour. He knew now what he had to do.

Monday, September 21, was a confused day. In her office Helen Kushnick found a letter from John Agoglia dismissing her from her job at NBC. She took it in to Jay Leno. He marched up the stairs to John Agoglia's office and told him he didn't agree with the firing. Then he walked out.

Later in the day, Jay Leno released a statement from his office regarding Helen Kushnick. In it, he said that he did not fully agree with the action NBC had taken in the termination of her contract. And he said that her departure seemed to be illogical in view of the fact that the show was continuing its history of success. He wound up stating that he supported Helen Kushnick.

Littlefield was in a quandary. This was all shadowplay. This was all P.R. hype—words, words, words. What would Jay *really* do? That was the burning question?

Jay came up for air. He cornered Littlefield. He pleaded with him, promising once again that he was going to do the show. He asked for Littlefield's help in getting through this messy situation. And he repeated once again that he was going to do the show.

Later Helen besieged Jay in his office, raging at him. Staffers nearby could hear the shouts and the screams. It was a day of horror and indecision. Helen raged through the offices, shouting out her ultimatums.

One. She refused to leave the show.

Two. If she was forced out, she would go.

Three. She would take Leno with her.

Helen finally retreated to her office and shut the door with an ear-splitting crash. Inside the office, staffers outside could hear bumps and screeches as of heavy furniture being moved. Objects were thrown against walls. Glass shattered again and again.

She finally left the Burbank studios at the end of the show's taping around 8 P.M. in what would be her final departure. In her office in the trash can lay glass shards from a framed Hirschfield sketch of Jay Leno.

But the main question still remained. Would the show go on past Monday? Actually, amidst the turmoil, the strife, the Sturm und Drang, Jay Leno pulled it all together, much like the professional showman he was, and managed to turn out one of his smoothest performances to date. It was an incredible achievement for a man being torn apart by the breakdown of long-established loyalties and feelings and dreams.

Helen's threat to take Jay Leno with her had proved empty in the final analysis. He was all ready to put in a hard day's work when he arrived at the studio on Tuesday, following Black Monday. Had Helen Kushnick really thought he would sacrifice his career for her sake? Leno's seventeen-year-old professional relationship with Helen Kushnick was over.

Leno reported to worried staffers huddling around the office that "something was wrong with Helen." He said that in spite of the fact that he now had no executive producer, he would continue to do the show. A big sigh of relief escaped most of his close associates.

At a press conference later, Leno said that he hoped to put in five or ten years as the steward of *The Tonight Show*. "I wouldn't be so presumptuous as to assume I would be doing it as long as Johnny. I think in this day and age it is probably not possible, but I would like to give it a long enough shot to be deemed successful. After all, I don't have anything else in mind. I mean, I'm not going to switch to modern interpretive dance!"

Warren Littlefield noted that he backed to the hilt Leno's decision to stay at *Tonight*. "Leno has proven extremely popular with the late-night audience, and we are confident that the show will continue its late-night dominance for many, many years."

When eventually the news of Kushnick's termination as executive producer of *The Tonight Show* was announced in the press about a week later, a great deal of the drama and near-hysteria of the event was over and forgotten.

Nevertheless Warren Littlefield admitted to the curious press that there were problems that had cropped up. "It wasn't as seamless a transition as we had hoped," he told the *New York Daily News*.

"Obviously, we had a problem and that was with the executive producer, so we made a change."

At his own request, Jay Leno was allowed to have his own say about the ouster. He made a short, rather unemotional statement to the effect that Helen Kushnick, his manager for seventeen years, had gotten what he called a "bad rap" from the network and that "sexism in Hollywood" was a contributing factor in her dismissal.

There had been no move to replace her, but Leno did not say anything about that. In fact, the assistant producer, Debbie Vickers, more or less took over the running of the show.

The story went on to say that in spite of Jay Leno's loyalty to Helen Kushnick, "some viewers think his on-air performance has improved since she left."

Littlefield echoed that sentiment in a tribute to Leno's growing talent as the host of *The Tonight Show.* "Look at the shows," he said. "Each and every night, Jay is only getting more relaxed, more comfortable. There's more of a connection with the studio audience and the talent on the show."

But he did not stop there.

"At a time when many people said it should have been utter chaos, and 'Let's watch the show fall apart,' people saw Jay Leno be as great as Jay Leno can be."

Helen Kushnick did not seek the psychiatric help a number of the NBC brass felt she needed. In fact, she seemed well able to take control of herself on her own. She and Leno had several conversations after they parted, all in the spirit of their long professional association.

Nevertheless, Leno was smarting at what he considered Helen's absolutely unacceptable handling of the planted *New York Post* story.

Worse than planting the story, to Jay Leno, was the fact that she had lied to him deliberately when he had asked her if she had anything to do with it. He had passed on the lie to Johnny Carson—who, of course, didn't believe the lie at all. Carson was still an icon in Jay's eyes. One did not tar and feather one's hero in order to promote one's job.

One of the first things he did when he arrived at the office on Tuesday—the day after the big blowup—was to telephone Johnny Carson and as abjectly as he could apologize to him for the lie he had told him all-unknowingly. Carson was his usual adroit self in accepting the apology and in pointing out to Jay Leno that in show business—as in life—things were not always as they seemed to be. The unstated point was that Jay Leno had obviously learned a lesson here and should be able to profit from it.

Once that was settled, Leno then telephoned Ken Kragen, the record company executive whose story to the *Los Angeles Times* had precipitated the Helen Kushnick debacle. Kragen was decent about Leno's apology, and in turn suggested that perhaps Helen Kushnick needed help of some kind. When Leno did not answer directly, Kragen decided not to press the point and simply assured Leno that things were on an even keel once again with him and NBC.

But Leno did not stop there. He found himself questioning certain things that had been suggested for upcoming shows when they were going over the schedule that day. If someone responded that the idea was Helen Kushnick's, Leno quickly began studying the concept in detail—and then usually dumped it.

Not *all* the concepts were jettisoned. But the majority of them were. In effect, what Jay Leno was doing was laundering *The Tonight Show* in his own way from the Kushnick touch. This habit would persist for months, until all suggestions and changes by Helen Kushnick were completely obliterated from the show.

No one protested.

As for the booking practices instigated by Helen Kushnick, they were definitely out of order under the new management. What had proved to be the undoing of the former executive producer now vanished entirely from *The Tonight Show*. Rules she had carefully enforced no longer existed. A much more relaxed attitude prevailed in the Burbank studios.

To Leno, the show had never looked better.

Recreation

Leno puts in a long day and night at work, which doesn't give him much time for his favorite hobby—tinkering with his legion of cars and motorcycles.

As Leno put it:

"A lot of guys here in Hollywood have one car and a lot of women. I have a lot of cars and one woman. It's a lot easier."

He wakes up at 7:00 A.M. after only four hours of sleep and never reaches his office in Burbank later than nine-thirty or ten. Once there, he studies his researchers' notes on the night's guests and listens to their music, watches their films, or reads their best-sellers. Meanwhile, he is working the phones and taking meetings.

At five thirty he tapes the hour-long show, which is a lead-pipe cinch, as far as Leno is concerned. "It looks easy because it is easy. Please! I used to wash cars for a living. Now that was hard."

At eight at night he usually arrives at his Benedict Canyon home in Beverly Hills. But his day isn't finished—not by a long shot. Then he prepares for the next night's monologue. At nine the *Tonight* writing staff of fourteen visits him. His wife, Mavis, retires for the night while Leno fixes up a late-night supper and commences to bat ideas for jokes around. This may take six-odd hours, with visitors rarely leaving before 3:00 A.M.

Back at his Burbank office in the morning, he works out for an hour on the treadmill in his dressing room, pen in hand, going over jokes, refining them, jotting down corrections on his monologue script.

"The really wonderful thing about the treadmill," Leno told *Runner's World* in 1994, "is being able to do two things at the same time. I love doing two things at the same time. I tried trail running, but I got five minutes out there and the only thing to do was . . . run."

From about 8:45 A.M.. to 9:45 A.M. Leno lifts weights under the guidance of his own personal trainer. Leno insists that the world of comedy is a dog-eat-dog one. "Comedy is a lot like going to the gym and working out. You have to do it every day to keep sharp. If I don't work out every day—if I don't stay sharp—then I lose my edge."

Furthermore, "I'm an example of success through persistence. I've gotten to where I am by getting out there every night and doing it. In school I wasn't a good student, but I got through it because I never missed a class. The reason I don't take a vacation is because I want to be ready to go when the other guy isn't. Sooner or later the other guy will want to take a vacation, and when he does, I'll be ready to take advantage of that."

Leno admits he is ambitious. "I'm driven, but my doctor says I have the lowest stress level of anyone over forty he's ever seen. My blood pressure is just a hundred over sixty." Much lower than that and he'd be a corpse. Leno avers he is not stressed out because he loves his job. "I never have any trouble getting up for a show."

His regimen of running has increased his stamina, so that he can endure long bouts with his competition. "I have much more energy than I used to have. I feel better. I feel stronger. I recently had my first check-up since I began running. My cholesterol was down, and I could go three times longer on the stress test than three years ago."

He hasn't always been a runner. He took it up in March 1994, probably because Letterman, who has become his main rival, was doing it, but Leno won't admit to that.

"I always sort of avoided working out before I got this job, mainly because I was always on the road. But now I have no excuse. Though I hate to say it, I'm in better shape at forty-four than I was at forty." The fact is, his lower metabolism, brought on by aging, increases the importance of running in his life. "I eat huge amounts of food. If I didn't work out, I'd weigh three or four hundred pounds."

Leno feels that telling jokes "really is a fun business to be in and it's a lot like exercising. I like doing my act. It's like working out at a gym an hour and fifteen minutes a night."

While exercising, he can think up jokes, such as this one about the one-time Bush administration, which, Leno claims, learned something from the Persian Gulf War: "The next time, have the war a little closer to the election."

Or what about this one?

"O.J. is not the kind of person we'd like to do [as a guest]. There's a lot of people we turn down—we turned down Joey Buttafuoco."

Or this one about his taking over *The Tonight Show*:

"This is like living with a woman for five years and then telling her parents you're getting married. They're not shocked—just relieved that it's finally working out."

Or:

"I can't handle any of the business side [of comedy]. I just am not interested in that. Show biz is like making love. You can like it a lot, but that doesn't mean you want to be a gynecologist."

Or:

"If it doesn't come in a cardboard box, I won't eat it."

Or the risky one about the Los Angeles riots:

"I just got back from entertaining the troops—on Hollywood Boulevard."

Or the one about his refusal to take a vacation:

"I'm not a vacation guy. . . . I mean, staying home would be wonderful [instead of traveling somewhere]. You know, the other day I was trying to make a phone call from my house, and I kept getting the wrong number. Beep. Beep. And I realized: I was pressing nine before I dialed the number. You know. I think I'm in a hotel."

When not lifting comedy weights, if he ever manages to have any free time, Leno spends the best part of it with his treasure trove of antiques and pricey cars and motorcycles. At last count he owned forty motorcycles.

Why motorcycles? "I've always been mechanical. I don't have anything against the Japanese bikes, but I do think they are a little too technical. For someone that likes to work on their motorcycles, that's a big turn-off. I like motorcycles that need me."

He enjoys discussing motorcycles on *The Tonight Show*. "Now, everybody has an opinion about motorcycles. Often on *The Tonight Show*, I'll bring up the subject, and no matter which way the discussion goes, I'll get a lot of mail on the subject, most of it supportive."

When motorcycling, he doesn't hang around with the celebrity crowd of Mickey Rourke, Sylvester Stallone, Gary Busey, Dan Aykroyd, James Caan, Patrick Swayze, Arnold Schwarzenegger, or their ilk. He prefers cycling by himself, a kind of rebel without a cause and without a following.

Among his motorcycle collection are a Harley Dresser, a Cagiva Paso, a Harley-Davidson FXRS Sport Edition, a Vincent Black Knight, and a Vincent Black Shadow. Each model has a V-twin engine, which he considers mandatory for a premium chopper.

"V-twins have always been what bikes are all about. Aesthetically, for width, for handling, low center of gravity, the V-twin always was the ideal way to go. It's the perfect bike engine."

His warehouse-sized garage sports a hydraulic lift which lowers his motorcycles to the basement, where Leno can putter around with them at his leisure. The walls of the garage are plastered with photos and posters of antique motorcycles. What little space remains is covered with thumbtacked letters from motorcycle clubs.

One of his most enjoyable activities is restoring old motorbikes, such as Brough Superiors, a BSA, a Honda CBX, and a couple of sixties-style Hondas. Restoring Japanese bikes doesn't give him a kick, for when you finish sprucing them up, they're worthless. "I try to buy stuff that's worth something from the start."

Before he loaded his bank account with megabucks, he had to buy cheaper motorcycles to match his smaller income. Nowadays, a millionaire many times over, he can afford the ne plus ultra of the chopper world, including a red-and-green Ducati Mike Hailwood Replica, a 750 MV Augusta Inline-Four, a 1970 Triumph Bonneville, and, his prize possession, a 1951 Vincent Black Shadow.

It is Leno's contention that a purring Ducati is music to the trained ear—"one of the most beautiful sounds" in the world. Even so, his favorite is still the Vincent Black Shadow. When he needs to focus his mind he'll venture into his garage and merely stare at the Vincent, perusing its nooks and crannies. "I just don't think there is a prettier motorcycle than the Vincent. It's truly a classic shape."

At the age of fourteen or so, he became the proud possessor of a Honda 90, his first motorcycle. "It was all busted up. It was in a field behind one of my friends' houses, and I think it had been thrown out by an angry parent or something."

It was, in plain English, a mess. "It didn't run. I mean, half the parts were missing. Of course, being the master mechanics that we neighborhood kids were, we took it apart and painted the piston red and painted the block blue—just everything wrong. It never ran, but we had a lot of fun sitting on it, pretending it ran."

It would be years later that Leno would own a motorbike that actually worked. "My first year in college I bought a secondhand [1970] Honda 350 from a Harley dealer. I used that for a while to get around until I could get a real bike."

In Los Angeles, the first motorcycle he owned was a Yamaha 650, a veritable piece of junk on wheels. The thing was so unpleasant

to ride that he almost decided to throw in the towel when it came
to bike riding. If it felt this bad, who needed it?

Then he bought a Honda Inline-Six CBX, which changed his
mind forever. This was what bike riding was all about. It handled
lousy and he had to bust a gut to maintenance it, but the way it
sounded compensated for all that. Furthermore, the controls operated, the bike offered a smooth ride, and it actually stopped when
he hit the brakes.

"With my old bikes, when you wanted to stop, you had to get
their attention first. It was like, 'Hey! Heyhey! Heyheyhey!
STOOOOP!' "

What intrigued him about the Honda was the fact that here
was a motorcycle as technically fascinating as any automobile. This
sudden revelation induced him to buy a Black Lightning for four
thousand dollars in 1977. The purchase turned out to be the beginning of his collection of classic antiques.

"I feel a special kinship with the Vincents," in which form
followed function to a T. The design represented the architect's
unique vision of motorbike as motorbike.

The new motorcycles cut no ice with Leno. They are too complex and lack distinction. "I think that one of the problems with
motorcycling today is that people get bored."

Whereas the new bikes are a flat-out bore to Leno, he relishes
tracking down old bikes, restoring them, and casting about for parts
to replace broken ones.

Each old chopper has a history behind it. "You can always associate a Vincent with the people who built it, much like people
associate Harley-Davidsons with Willy G."

Leno refuses to allow mechanics to work on his bikes. The only
time he will let them touch them is if he himself can't repair the

machine. After all, he's a professional comedian, not a professional mechanic. "I do one thing well. I tell jokes, so when I have a serious problem, I take my bike to some friends. I'm almost embarrassed that I don't work with my hands when I am around these guys, because they are so *good* with machines."

Not a speed demon, Leno likes a slow, manageable bike he can ride to the local post office with his helmet and black leather togs on. The modern motorcycles are designed to be driven fast, which turns Leno off. He isn't trying to win a race, he's trying to relax when he rides.

Leno, the motorcycle fiend, has ridden a bike onto the David Letterman show and has also participated as ceremonial parade master for the Southern California Love Ride, a hundred-mile trek staged to raise funds for the Muscular Dystrophy Association.

At the head of that motorcade of bikes, he joked to the 1,300 riders, "Yeah, if any of you guys are on *Japanese* bikes, don't worry, we'll have someone to help you out."

Another bike that gets pride of place in his collection, along with the Vincent Black Shadow, is his 1938 Brough Superior SS100. He calls it the Brough (rhymes with *rough*). Its mammoth 1,000-cc V-twin has double fishtail chrome pipes jutting out the right side like twin clarinets.

Every weekend he makes a point of riding the Brough, showing it off. "I love going past some guys, going out to the Rock Store. I'll deliberately pull up alongside some guy on a Gold Wing, make a face at him, and pass him on the outside. Maybe it's because I'm in show business? That's the fun of owning the thing, *riding* it. I've put a lot of miles on the Brough. I take it to the club [the Rock Store] and park it on the street."

According to Leno, Lawrence of Arabia, né T. E. Lawrence,

used to ride Brough Superiors. He was so fond of them he rode one
to his death in an accident; Leno has a toolbox that bears a brass
plate with the inscription "A skittish motorcycle with a touch of
blood in it is better than all the riding animals on earth."

Not that Leno is a Hell's Angel. Far from it. "Well, the people
I ride with are not stereotypical bikers. I mean, we don't go down-
town and beat up homos."

He was once asked by a curious talk-show host why he kept
forty motorbikes on his premises.

Leno: "Suppose I suddenly wreck one of my bikes? I've got to
have something to drive when I'm fixing the wrecked one."

Not only does Leno own a host of motorcycles, he owns thirty
cars as well.

As he tells it, "I got my first car when I was thirteen or fourteen.
Actually, it was a 1934 Ford V-8 truck, which I got running and
restored so I'd have something to drive when I turned sixteen."

His first new car was "a 1965 Buick Gran Sport with a 401-
cubic-inch V-8 and four-speed transmission. I think I was the only
kid in high school with a brand-new Buick. I always liked to work,
so I'd saved up for it by working after school."

He is the proud possessor of a '67 and '70 Lamborghini Kiura,
a V-32 Packard V12, an '89 Bentley Turbo R, an '86 Countach, a
'54 Jaguar XK120M, a 427 Cobra, a '46 Morgan three-wheeler, a
1915 Hispano-Suiza with an 18.5-liter French Spad aircraft engine,
a Delahaye, a Bugatti, a Dodge Viper, and, not to be left out, his
much-coveted (for sentimental reasons) Buick Roadmaster. He even
has a "bunch of Stanley Steamers."

He has been known to drive his steam cars to work. "Steamers have lots of power. A 1909 Stanley develops 700 foot-pounds of torque (compared with 340 foot-pounds for a 1995 Corvette). I recently got a 1934 Rolls-Royce with a 27-liter Merlin aircraft engine. So now the Hispano is my wife's car."

Each of his cars appeals to him for different reasons, mainly based on his mood at the moment. "I just did the brakes on my Morgan, so I'm having a lot of fun with that right now. There's a car you don't have to be going ninety miles an hour in to appreciate."

He feels cars should mirror the designer's personality, as should motorcycles. Today's cars, sadly, don't fill the bill, as they are designed by a "committee" system.

"I tend to like both Italian and British machinery," says Leno. One wonders if this is so because his father was Italian and his mother Scottish. "Italians try to cram as much horsepower as they can into their cars." He considers British cars "charming" on account of their eccentricity.

He goes on, "I guess what I've always loved about old cars, among other things, is that they're primarily mechanical rather than electrical."

One of the undesirable characteristics about new cars is that they can't be repaired. "With these new cars, you've got a sealed black box that must be replaced by another sealed black box." The subject of cars brings to mind another Leno anecdote about his childhood. When he got fired from his job at Wilmington Ford at the age of sixteen, he wrote a letter to Ford Motor Company Chairman Henry Ford II:

"One of my jobs was removing hubcaps to prevent kids from stealing them at night. One day I'm carrying a load of hubcaps . . . and drop a few because I come across the dealership's new general manager, who made me nervous. He says, 'You can't treat our property that way! You're fired!' I was so ashamed I pretended to go to work every day. It wasn't fair, so I wrote to Henry Ford II, telling what happened—and how I'd made my dad buy a 1964 Ford Galaxie 500 XL and a Ford sedan with a 7-liter (hot rod) V-8—and that my mother drove a Ford Falcon. About two weeks later, the dealership's owner called and said, 'Geez, I don't know who you know in Detroit, but you can have your old job back.' "

Cars are on his mind so much that he does jokes about them regularly, like this one:

"Years ago, if you wanted to kill yourself with a 1957 Chevy, you'd sit in the garage for fifteen minutes and you'd be dead. With today's cars, you're in that garage for six hours, and you're still not dead. The public doesn't realize how 'clean' today's cars are."

When Leno was able to move from his Hollywood Hills ranch house to his Beverly Hills mansion thanks to his monster paychecks as host of *The Tonight Show,* he had to drive all of his cars one at a time to the new mansion. Mavis would drive him back to the ranch house in her car each time so that he could pick up the next car. He has so many cars that the process took all of one day.

He finished transporting his museum of cars at three-thirty in the morning. Then he returned to the ranch house, disinterred Mavis's dead cat, took it to the manse, buried it there, grabbed two hours of sleep, and arrived at the airport at 7:00 A.M., punctual as ever, ready to fly to his next gig.

He likes to work on *The Tonight Show,* but it's not his whole life. "I have fun here, I enjoy it and I have a good time, but I don't fall in love with it: It's not my life. I have a wife and a life that I really enjoy, and if push comes to shove, I would know what to choose."

He wishes he could discuss cars with Letterman, as Letterman is also a car fanatic. In 1995, Leno said, "I would love to talk cars with Dave sometime. I know he knows cars and has some really good ones. It's just awkward now. I did call him a couple years ago and asked him about a Daytona Ferrari, and we talked a little bit about cars. . . . You know, I would love to have the opportunity to make Dave laugh again. And vice versa. But now it's just so odd."

One of Leno's classic anecdotes deals with a motorcycle adventure he had with his friend Gene Braunstein. He's told it so many times over that it has the distinction now of never being the same yarn twice. And this was not only a classic anecdote, but a classic adventure in biking as well—all taking place in crazy Los Angeles.

It was 1986 or thereabouts. He and Gene were riding their motorcycles on Mulholland Drive in the Hollywood Hills. Stopping for a rest, Leno dismounted from his Harley-Davidson, and Braunstein followed suit.

In the darkness, they took in the breathtaking sight of the lighted Los Angeles basin at their feet in the distance. Mesmerized by the necklaces of street lights that wound beneath them, Leno was suddenly taken aback at the feeling of a cold steel ring thrust into the nape of his neck. It felt like the muzzle of a gun. He wanted to turn around but was afraid of the consequences.

"You're trying to rob my house!" said the gun-bearer in a no-nonsense voice.

Leno's throat was so dry he could barely swallow, let alone talk. Frightened that the assailant would become angrier if he did not answer, he contrived to squeak, "What are you talking about? I'm riding my bike!" His normal high-pitched Mickey Mouse voice now sounded like Mickey Mouse on helium.

"You bikers are all thieves," growled the man. Doing a slow burn, he ranted on. "You bikers are all thieves! A biker robbed my house last week!"

No wonder the guy was upset. Lost in his troubled thoughts, he realized a woman was standing unseen in the darkness and talking to the bushwhacker. She wanted him to leave Leno alone and return to their car.

The guy shrugged her off and jammed the gun muzzle deeper into Leno's neck. "I'll give you two minutes—you hear that?—two minutes to clear out of here and never come back!"

As though Leno would want to meet up with this nut in the dark again.

The man stole off into the darkness, gunned his unseen car's motor, and peeled off.

Leno and Braunstein, distressed by their ordeal, made tracks out of there.

But that wasn't the end of it.

Six months later, Leno was shopping at a ritzy supermarket in Beverly Hills when he heard a voice summoning his attention.

"Jay! Jay! Remember me?"

Leno studied the speaker. He couldn't place him. Just another shopper.

"My wife yelled at me for pulling a gun on you!" explained the man.

Now Leno recognized the voice, which he had wished he would never have the misfortune to hear again, thank you.

"We saw you on television," the guy babbled on, as if he and

Leno were good buddies. "We're so excited that you were the guy I held at gunpoint!"

Uh-oh, thought Leno, deciding he should beat a strategic retreat—

"Hey! Would it be possible for you to autograph this box of cereal for me? Gee. . . ."

A puzzled Larry King one night asked Jay Leno what kind of pleasure he actually got out of his thirty automobiles.

"Let me tell you this," Leno ad-libbed on the spot. "I have never gotten crabs from an automobile."

Leno's *Tonight* Format

Under Jay Leno, *The Tonight Show* was basically a new show with a new host and a new cast of characters. Nevertheless, the general trappings of the "old" show—Johnny Carson's version of the *Tonight Show*—remained firmly in place. It was as if Jay Leno had gone to a tailor and asked for a completely new wardrobe; the tailor obliged him by simply cutting and sewing together a brand-new suit exactly like the one he had come in with.

Yes, it was a new show. And yes, it was the old show all over again, polished up a bit, its personnel changed, and a new sound acquired. But basically it was the same old show that Jay Leno had been doing once a week in his stint as permanent guest host for some time now.

The general shape of the show was the same, with small innovations here and there. It fell into three main parts:

1. The stand-up monologue at the show's beginning.
2. The musical background and the visiting band(s) or group(s).
3. The interviews with guests.

The monologue usually took up five to ten minutes at the beginning. The musical background continued throughout the hour-long show. The visiting musical groups took up the regular amount of time for one number, perhaps two, or very occasionally three, depending on the group and on the time schedule. The speaking guests took up the remainder of the hour. What looked like some forty-five minutes actually boiled down to less than thirty with the commercials spliced in.

Of course, there was plenty of time left for the kind of skits Johnny Carson used to do in his various characterizations: Carnac, for example. But Jay Leno did not have a large repertoire of characters; in fact, in the beginning he did not have any. These were to be developed as the show progressed. As usual Leno went to his strength—the stand-up monologue—honing that to perfection before moving on to other innovations.

The major portion of the show was given over to its interviews, although the majority of its success lay in the monologue—both of which fell to Jay Leno. But indeed the musical part of the show was certainly an important and integral part of its brilliance and pizzazz. And music was Leno's first consideration in dressing the show up and addressing his own needs and desires.

*　　*　　*

From the first, it was obvious to Jay that he would not be following Johnny Carson in *all* his mannerisms, routines, content, and number of entertainers on the show.

Leno had worked on his own for his entire career. No props. No partners. No second bananas. That meant that there would be no Ed McMahon, Carson's announcer, to sit by him after the standup, and breeze through a few short conversational breaks about this and that. That meant that there would be no Doc Severinsen, Carson's bandleader, to act as a target for Carson's one-liners or ad-lib masterpieces when they chanced to surface.

It was obvious that the Severinsen band would be leaving. And so Jay Leno put his mind to the thought of what kind of a musical background he should be trying to get for his show. He knew that many had criticized Carson for using a band like Doc Severinsen's—strictly a pickup outfit that played numbers people knew by heart and wanted to hear over again. He also knew that he could not go as far as Arsenio Hall in getting together a jazz band of the kind Hall sported. And he did not want a rock band of the type that entertained the viewers of the David Letterman show.

He wanted something different.

In looking around he finally spotted the right man. He was an up-and-coming black jazz saxophonist called the cornerstone of the American jazz renaissance—a man named Branford Marsalis. From New Orleans, the perfect place for the perfect jazz aficionado, Branford Marsalis was a younger brother of Wynton Marsalis, a trumpeter and leader of a jazz quintet of some fame.

Marsalis had not played forever with his brother, but had branched out by backing up pop star Sting, and then he even appeared in several films of Spike Lee and Danny DeVito. He was

featured on albums with Dizzy Gillespie and Public Enemy, and
had a number of his own albums out.

It was Bobby Colomby, a drummer for Blood, Sweat & Tears,
who suggested Marsalis to Jay Leno, and Leno did some appropriate
research on Marsalis and finally talked to him. Jay could see that
Marsalis was a master at jazz stylings. What could be better for Jay
Leno, the new star of *Tonight*, than to have a new band that was
truly a jazz band of distinction? That would surely bring in some
of the younger viewers, which seemed to be the main thing the
network bosses wanted.

Branford was only thirty-one when, on December 12, 1991, he
was officially signed up to replace Doc Severinsen as the leader of
the *Tonight* band. Indeed, Branford would not only be replacing
Severinsen, but Ed McMahon as well, since part of his job would
be to act as a kind of foil to Jay Leno's hosting role.

"He's incredibly charismatic," Leno told *The New York Times
Magazine*. "The first time I met this guy, I realized he was somebody who could say in four words what most people took twenty-
five or thirty words to say. Most people new to TV, maybe they
stick their face in the camera, you have to pry them away. But
Branford, you want to put his face in front of the camera. We decided, 'Let's push Branford, let's make him an important part of
the show.'"

In effect, Branford Marsalis became the Number Two man on
Tonight.

Leno's analysis of Branford was right on the button. What he
saw as Branford's ability to use few words to express himself, and
his lack of desire to hog the camera, were two attributes that were
later to come under fire as definite disadvantages that hurt rather

than helped his performance as Number Two man. And they had nothing to do with his jazz abilities at all.

Right away, while the show was getting shaped up and put together, Marsalis composed a new theme song—to take the place of the Johnny Carson theme that Paul Anka had written.

Marsalis: "It's not a swing tune at all. A swing tune doesn't reflect Jay. When you look at Jay, jazz doesn't come to mind either. It's just a tune that reflects Jay."

The band was finally organized and featured big-time talents like pianist Kenny Kirkland, drummer Jeff "Tain" Watts, bassist Bob Hurst, trombonist Matt Finders, trumpeter Sal Marquex, percussionist Vicki Randle, and guitarist Kevin Eubanks.

Marsalis was in seventh heaven, or at least he acted as if he were. "I'm just happy and honored to have a band with some of the greatest musicians in the world in it. It's a pleasure." He was astounded that he had been given such leeway in selecting the men and women he thought best in the field.

The band leader endorsed Leno's commitment to top-drawer entertainment. "Jay's a special person. And the philosophy of the show is to get the very best people, the best of the best in the entertainment world. Not the most popular, but the best."

Critics were receptive to the combination of Leno's squeaky clean image and Marsalis's cool, engaging personality.

Like most musicians, Marsalis had played a road circuit prior to his gig with *The Tonight Show*. He enjoyed the chance to work at a steady job rather than always have to be running for the next train or jetliner and the next job.

"I needed a situation where I can wake up in the same bed as I did the morning before." Twelve years of touring with his trumpeter brother Wynton and rock-and-roller Sting had just about worn him out.

The *Tonight Show* would be no walk in the park for him, though. Marsalis had his work cut out for him. He had to arrive at the NBC Burbank studios by 1:00 P.M. and remain well past midnight every weekday.

He did not let the crème-de-la-crème job go to his head. "It's just another job. If you look at it any other way, you lose your objectivity."

But to him, television took second place to jazz and performing with legendary jazzman Sonny Rollins and with other musical luminaries.

Marsalis never considered the Arsenio Hall show competition for *The Tonight Show* and he said so. "I don't think there's really a competition. It's really like apples and oranges. It's just a different show."

When he hired Marsalis, Leno was over the moon about his musical background. "Now, you have essentially high-tech TV with stereo, which is almost as good as FM radio. So music plays a bigger role."

As the show revved up to speed during May and June and July, the music came over very well. Most people seemed to like it. It *was* jazz done by experts in the classical style of jazz—modified by the taste of the 1990s, but it was the real thing. Nobody really complained about the music. It was pop music with jazz stylings, not jazz with pop stylings.

An important difference to the musical director.

However, the byplay between Jay Leno and Branford Marsalis seemed to grate on some viewers. Leno liked to turn to Branford every so often, more or less to include him and his band in with the show, but at the same time to establish a link between the two men. A link between Number One and Number Two. And that was where the trouble came in.

The greatest of all comedians—Johnny Carson—could always do better with a joke that bombed than with a joke that scored. He could twist and turn things around until the laugh he got by his barbed ad libs was far superior to the joke as originally written.

Leno tried that with Marsalis. When a joke visibly died without a murmur from the audience, Jay would turn to Marsalis. "Do you think that joke is funny?"

Now the answer he wanted, of course, was "no." But he also wanted *something more*—a comment that he could play with, develop into a kind of phoenix of a joke, one that could rise from the ashes and get the laugh after all.

Unfortunately, when Marsalis responded with a *no,* he *meant* it. His *no* became a criticism of the entire department of the show concerned with writing the jokes. It reflected on the show as well as on the men who told the jokes.

"Sometimes it looked as if we were bumping heads," Leno said. "A lot of times on the show I'd say, 'Branford, is this funny?' He'd go, 'Oh no, man. That's not funny at all.' Which would make me laugh. I mean, I enjoy Branford's sarcasm. But on the air it came across as something else."

In fact, the viewers were confused. Some felt that the band leader was putting down the star of the show

"After a while, I said, 'You know, Branford, maybe you should, like, fake a laugh or something.' He'd go, 'Well, I don't like to fake laughs.' I said, 'Well, I don't know, we got to come up with something.' "

Marsalis was appalled. He was a musician. Yes, he had agreed to talk on the show, but more or less as a kind of permanent guest. He did not feel that being dishonest in his role as leader of the band was right; it made his music suspect somehow. It was as if he felt the integrity of real jazz was being questioned by a comic trying to get a boffo laugh out of *him*.

This stiffness between Leno and Marsalis grew and the exchanges became fewer and further between. Leno always kept the smile on his face and never put Marsalis down in front of an audience, but he did wonder exactly where they were going with all of this.

Leno had never wanted his announcer to take over the second banana spot as Ed McMahon had done; he thought such an arrangement would be much too close to the format of the Johnny Carson show. And so when he went looking for an announcer, he selected a person who could do a lot of different voices, to be used in the skits and other things that would be prepared as comedy bits on the show.

In January 1992, he and Helen Kushnick interviewed a number of announcers and finally settled on a man named Edd Hall. Hall had worked on *Get a Life* and *Married . . . with Children* and had served as a graphic designer for *Late Night with David Letterman*. In his earlier years, he had been a page for *Saturday Night Live*. He had worked for Home Box Office, for Showtime, and for the Learning Channel.

He had at least 150 different voices—just as Lon Chaney had a hundred or more different faces. He did not mind not being on camera all the time, and rather liked being in control of voice-over comments where he could change his voice at will to invent different characters.

"I don't mind being behind the camera," he told *People* magazine. "I am basically a lazy guy."

Hall met his wife, Liza, when he was working at NBC. She was working at a nearby Lindy's restaurant. The two of them moved to the Los Angeles area in 1990 so Hall could pursue announcing and voice-over work full-time in Hollywood. There, his wife became a talent manager.

About his work for Letterman, Hall said, "At the time, that was the only job open. I took it because the Letterman show was so cool, and Dave used us a lot. I knew I'd be getting acting jobs out of it, both on-camera and voice. Dave called me a 'late-night tough guy.' "

At fourteen, Hall had been a teenage disc jockey in Corning, New York, where he grew up. His name, Edd, was really Ed. He had added the extra *d* just for the fun of the thing.

"There are advantages to being just a voice and not a face on television," he joked. "I can go to Bagel Nosh and not be recognized."

Hall's stepfather, Bill Hall, said that Hall's apparent modesty was a heavy smoke screen. "Don't let him kid you. When he gave us his new phone number, he told us not to release it to anyone—the words of a true rising star."

One of Jay Leno's specific peculiarities was the fact that he wanted to write *all* his own material. He could do that when he traveled around the country doing various gigs in different places. But now, using up a group of standup gags every night of the working week, he needed much more material than he had been able to come up with all by himself.

And so he started a search for a group of writers—much like the stable Johnny Carson had developed over the years and used behind that well-known desk. Since becoming guest host, Leno had used gags that were sent in to him by various professional gag writers, and he began talking to these men and women about joining him in Hollywood.

Many wanted to retain their freedom. Also, many didn't want to live in L.A. It's tough place to survive. But Jay did manage to get a number of free-lancers to come to Hollywood, and through recommendations, he got other people to join up. In the end there were about a dozen writers on the staff, with Leno titled head writer.

These writers were: Jimmy Brogan, Brad Dickson, Wayne Kline, Jon Macks, Joe Medeiros, Ron Richards, John Romeo, Peter Sears, Marvin Sibermintz, and Buddy Winston.

To round out her staff, Helen Gorman Kushnick, the executive producer, had two assistant producers named Debbie Vickers and Bill Royce.

Of course, that was only during the first four months of the show, following which she was fired.

One of the most difficult things Leno had been required to do when he took over as guest host for Johnny Carson back in 1987 was to get his interviewing style down pat. He had always worked with jokes that stood on their own. The people involved in the jokes were at some distance from Leno—out there somewhere in space.

Or they were names that were good for a laugh no matter what you said about the people.

Leno found it hard to zero in on the people he was talking to. He liked to write his own questions, to keep them in mind, and ask them when the guest had finished answering another one. Somehow there was a distance always between Leno and his interviewees. And it came across so strongly on camera that many viewers understood it as an inability on his part to relate to—connect with—the person he was talking to.

He had worked hard to get into the proper mode for interviewing—to make the Q.-and-A.s seem like parts of a continuing dialogue rather than an abrupt question-and-answer session that would remind viewers of a cop grilling a suspect. In fact, the style of sitdown interview Jay Leno was developing was quite similar to his stand-up comedy style. He did tend to simper some, but he did not overdo it. He did not rush in for the jugular at all; rather, he sat back and simply put on an understanding and empathetic air. He had learned long ago how to listen. The best comments he made were usually the result of a statement made by the person he was interviewing.

"The key [to a good interviewing style] is to listen to what people say, for something to turn around," he told Elvis Mitchell in a *Fresno Bee* interview.

For example, John Davidson was visiting Leno one night when he mentioned in an offhand fashion: "I do the *Miss World Show,* but it means nothing."

There were warning bells jangling in Leno's mind. Nevertheless, he felt compelled to sit up straighter and look at Davidson. "So you're doing *this* because it means nothing." It was a statement from Leno, not a question. And an unsettling one.

Davidson got the point. He flushed deeply and swallowed hard. The interview went on. But Leno had him right where he wanted him with that slip of the tongue.

Even if he tried, Leno might not be the best adversarial interviewer in the world. "I like hosting," he admitted, "because it's the only job in show business that means anything to me. By that, I mean it's a job that was there when I started in show business and it's still there—it's like stepping into a long-running play."

One night Leno had on Ahmad Rashad, the former professional football player for the Minnesota Vikings. In truth, Leno had always had a distaste for organized sports of any kind—the team effort thing—but he did not let any of this show when he chatted with Rashad. He was gentle and polite, typically Jay Leno on his best behavior.

Without realizing it, Leno let the talk drift around to children. And of course Rashad asked him the usual question: "Do you have any?"

"No, I don't," Leno answered quickly. "Maybe after the show tonight."

It was a joke. The audience laughed. So did Rashad. But the joke was a veil for something else. Leno was most sensitive about discussing personal details on the show. In addition, he had noticed that the audience's interest was beginning to flag during the Rashad interview. His joke served two purposes: to get Rashad back to football, and to get away from the too personal.

There are always temptations. "I mean," he told the *Calgary Herald,* "it's fun to do a show like this and have these attractive women come out, and you go, 'Oooooh!' Like Tori Spelling comes on the other night. Did you see that skirt she had on?" During a commercial break she said to Leno: "You know, I'm not wearing any underwear." Leno sighed. "That's about as far as it goes. In your mind you can do whatever you want. But if you take it any further than that, you're dead! So you just learn to keep things at a distance and have a good time."

Running around the country doing three hundred gigs a year had taught Leno to keep his head screwed on right. "If you go on the road and all twenty-five hundred seats are sold, well, you must be doing *something* right. If only three hundred seats are sold, you're probably doing something wrong. That's really the way you have to judge it."

Leno avoided topical humor in his interviews as much as he could. The problem with such references was that in many cases the audience was not able to keep up with him. Leno once said that he thought it took people at least a full day to sort of ingest something to the point where you could make a joke about it.

"I had a bunch of jokes the other week about Donald Trump going out with that Italian model. I put the monologue together, and *that day* Trump announced he was engaged to Marla Maples.

"So I took those jokes out, and that night I did a couple of jokes about him being engaged to Marla, and I could sense the studio audience didn't *believe* me. They've been on vacation, they've been waiting in line all day, and they said, 'What?' It didn't get much of a laugh. Whereas the next night it *did*, because they *believed* me. They'd heard it in the news."

Leno always knew he was the luckiest guy in the world when he finally got a contract to do *The Tonight Show*. He said that no one had ever come up to him and said: "Okay, listen, you're going to have to have a certain amount of ratings." And nobody said, "Jay, we've checked your demographics and you're very low with immature men between eleven and fourteen."

No. He was simply expected to come to the studio and fill in, do his best, and not worry about anything. He figures that he got the job because he had the right attitude. And since that attitude worked so well, he figured he'd continue to feel the same way about it.

Leno had never promised to hype anybody's work if he didn't truly think it was a good job. When he had on Jackie Collins, the writer of Hollywood sex potboilers and sister of actress Joan Collins, she became upset with him when he told her off-camera that he had not read her current book because he couldn't stand the genre.

"I told her I was sure she was a very nice person and I would hold up the book, but I was not going to say, 'My next guest is a wonderful writer.' It's like Harold Robbins. He is *not* a good author. He writes *Penthouse* letters that are very long. It's stupid. I hate it."

During his years as guest host on *The Tonight Show,* Jay had developed a special routine completely divorced from his stand-up jokes and his anecdotes. This was a routine that stemmed from the fact that he read the newspapers every day and kept up on the latest news all the time.

If Leno's stand-up one-liners were jokes on purpose, the jokes for this routine could definitely be called jokes by accident. It was an interesting gimmick—but one that you had to study carefully in order to get the joke. In a way, it was television's version of those fillers that used to appear in *The New Yorker* magazine at the end of the articles and stories—usually typos that were hilarious when read correctly.

Leno's version of *The New Yorker* fillers was an ingenious one. He'd clip the story, usually a small one with a big, easily read headline, blow it up, mount it on a board, and put it in front of the camera. The headline had to be something obviously ridiculous or laughable as it stood—a non sequitur, perhaps, a dangling participle maybe, a nonsensical statement, or an obvious blooper of one kind or another, even a typo if it was easy to spot.

A typical sampling of one of the headlines might be this one:

GAS CHAMBER EXECUTIONS MAY BE HEALTH HAZARD

Another was even sillier:

RESEARCHERS CALL MURDER A THREAT TO PUBLIC HEALTH

On that second one, Leno had a comment to make as he held the headline up for the audience to read. "How long did this study take?" he asked. "Do you think it was more than ten minutes?"

On the silly side might be a headline like this one:

UNEMPLOYMENT NOT WORKING, CRITICS SAY

With no comment at all.

Or:

DEATH IN THE RING: MOST BOXERS ARE NOT THE SAME AFTERWARD

Which prompted Leno to comment, "Yeah, I hear some of them are actually smarter."

For the typically flaky headline that seems to be a definite impossibility, how about this one?

SKIING SEASON OPENS IN IRAN

That one had Jay's comment immediately: "When I think of a skiing vacation I think of three places: Vail . . . Aspen . . . Tehran." Another one read:

LIVING TOGETHER LINKED TO DIVORCE

Soon enough the public caught on and joined in on the fun, sending in headlines week after week to Jay for use on the show. He was inundated at first with the TWO-HEADED MONSTER SEDUCES VIRGIN BATHER ON NUDE BEACH—and Leno soon put a stop to the submission of tabloid weeklies sold at the supermarket checkouts, in which the headlines are deliberately steamed up to *be* sensational or quirky.

The submissions were limited to regular dailies—which usually didn't contain the most amusing headlines—neighborhood papers and small-town weekly newspapers with select, intimate circulations. Those last two seemed to be breeding grounds for good reading:

TREES CAN BREAK WIND

BRAILLE DICTIONARY FOR SALE. MUST SEE TO APPRECIATE!

Or here's one that gets a laugh because of the fractured diction in the writing of the headline:

BAN ON NUDE DANCING ON GOVERNOR'S DESK

Or this one:

FAMILY CATCHES FIRE JUST IN TIME, CHIEF SAYS

Because of the popularity of the headline routine, Leno became the "author" of four books—*Headlines; More Headlines;* and *Headlines III: Not the Movie, Still the Book.* The fourth was a bit different, titled *Jay Leno's Police Blotter: Real-Life Crime Headlines.*

All profits from the first three books, incidentally, go to Helen Kushnick's Samuel Jared Kushnick Foundation (for AIDS research). Profits from the fourth go to the JDM Foundation, which funds various charity programs. There are several headlines also in the fourth book:

MAN GETS LIFE IN PRISON FOR RUNNING DRUG RING FROM PRISON

Leno's comment: "Talk about job security!"

The routine was one of the first features aside from Leno's stand-up monologue that was a part of the show's "new" format—except, of course, that it wasn't *new* at all, since Leno had used it himself numerous times when he was guest host on *Tonight.*

Up for Grabs

No sooner had the dust settled in the Burbank studios after the Helen Kushnick affair in September 1992 had been finally laid to rest than other, creepier, and more scary whispers began circulating through the building. During the Kushnick contretemps David Letterman's situation re *The Tonight Show* had been all but forgotten. But the Letterman thing was in no way dead; in fact, it was, if the rumors were correct, about to surface once again.

The first *big* buzz was an eye-opener indeed. David Letterman, the scuttlebutt had it, was now a client of one of the most powerful men in Hollywood—Michael Ovitz, chairman of Creative Artists Agency, a well-known stable of megastars in the show-biz world. The rumor was soon confirmed. David Letterman had opted to join the Hollywood power game, and had put himself in the hands of one of its master builders.

Jay Leno was unsurprised at the fact that CBS seemed to be wooing Letterman strongly; it was an obvious move for the embattled network to try to work itself into the late-night arena. After all, once they had been wooing Jay Leno! ABC was in the wings, too, even though they had Ted Koppel at the scene already, beating out the talk-show people with his political insights. Fox was wooing Letterman. So was Paramount, which syndicated Arsenio Hall's show, and there were others as well. Warner was in the field. Chris-Craft, the luxury boat marketers, wanted him for promotions. And also Disney and Viacom.

Even so, there was action a lot closer than those formidable giants of the industry. It was a much bruited-about fact that David Letterman did not particularly want to go to CBS and do a talk show opposite *The Tonight Show.* What he wanted was what he had always wanted: *The Tonight Show* on NBC. Ah, yes, but that show had gone to Jay Leno.

Or—had it?

The reason for the rumors and the covert negotiations was the pesky fact of Letterman's contract. He was fully tied up with NBC until the middle of 1993. There was not much he could do about it until that date was past. Of course, the rumor mills continued to grind; what he wanted NBC to do was alter his contract and include *The Tonight Show* in it!

There were other distractions as well. Because of the lucrative late-night mother lode, a lot of comics, conversationalists, and professional talkers were staking it out for mining. One of these newcomers, Dennis Miller, had already been closed down after only a seven-month trial. But there was Whoopi Goldberg in the future, it was said, who would join the talk-fest with a half-hour dialogue each night. Then, for the far future, there was the formidable actor Chevy Chase, whose schedule was set for September 1993.

And certainly there would be others.

In early December 1992 the story broke in *The New York Times* News Service that David Letterman had accepted CBS's offer for a talk show to run opposite *The Tonight Show with Jay Leno*. Letterman would be paid about $16 million a year; he would own the show; he would be able to produce a second late-night program to follow his own.

But the kicker to the story lay in a second paragraph, which said simply: "NBC now has thirty days to match or better the CBS offer, one of the richest in television history."

It was clear to Jay Leno that the CBS offer really did not settle anything. It was obvious that Letterman wanted *The Tonight Show*. He had said so many times already. He had indicated to Michael Ovitz that that was his primary desire.

And that meant that nothing could be counted on until the thirty-day period had passed.

Jay Leno did what he had done before. He went to the print media for help. He called *The New York Times* on December 22, just a few days before Christmas, with his tale of woe. No one, he told Bill Carter, had told him a thing about how the negotiations between Letterman and NBC were going. Was NBC considering meeting the offer proffered by CBS? Would Jay Leno be out of work?

He was, he said, surprised and disappointed with the NBC executives. He had expected better treatment from them in a situation like this. He was actually being threatened with losing his show to David Letterman even though he was fully contracted to do the show. Besides that, the show was doing all right in the ratings! Why change hosts?

The gist of Leno's complaint to Carter was the fact that nothing in the television business seemed to make any sense. For example, Leno's ratings were on their way up, the advertisers were in a good mood, and the affiliates were happy. But no one had said anything reassuring to Jay about not being dropped in favor of Letterman on January 15, the end of the crucial thirty-day period.

Covering one possibility in his conversation, Leno told Carter that he would refuse to do a show at 12:30 A.M. if they moved Letterman to the *Tonight Show* spot. And if the show went to Letterman, Leno would walk. In fact, he'd walk directly to the "other network"—CBS—if they asked him.

Even if Leno survived this threat to his job, he was losing credibility with the network executives he was working with—simply because the top brass apparently had doubts about his abilities and even his Q-factor.

Leno reminded Carter that he still had a hell of a lot of respect for Letterman. He repeated his off-stated tribute to Letterman that he would not have the job at *Tonight* if it weren't for David Letterman. He said he would do anything he could do to keep Letterman at NBC.

Short of giving up *The Tonight Show,* of course.

Leno admitted that NBC had put itself into an impossible position. However, he went on, the idea of "fragging your own soldier doesn't make any sense to me."

In spite of the indecision in the network front office, Jay Leno did not really believe that NBC would pull the plug on him. And yet, of course, the annoying thing was that he couldn't even be sure about that!

*   *   *

In the end it was actually the final deal NBC put on the table that was not totally pleasing to David Letterman. He would get *The Tonight Show,* yes. But he would not get it until May 1994, a year and a half in the future, simultaneous with the windup of Jay Leno's current contract. There were other considerations to study, as well. It was obvious that the NBC brass had not conducted themselves with the utmost sensitivity during the Letterman negotiations. They had apparently overlooked the fact that he might actually have wanted to do *The Tonight Show.*

Their handling of David Letterman—a man who had made them millions of dollars already—had all been pretty slipshod. Nor was the handling of Jay Leno done with any greater finesse or acumen. In fact, both men were really left twisting in the wind.

Leno recalled the situation later on: "You sort of hear rumors. You're at the catering truck and you hear, 'Oh, Mr. Leno, I'm sorry to hear about—' Pause. 'What?' 'Well, you know, the—you know, the chief said today you had some problems.' 'He did? Well, what did he say?' 'Oh, you know—you know, he had heard from—' 'What? What are you talking about?' 'Corporations. Rumor, rumor, rumor, rumor. You know.' "

And then when he finally did get the call—and he got it—it was even worse than the rumor mill had implied it would be. The call: "Jay, we don't know what we're going to do. That's our honest answer."

Jay: "Okay, I believe you. Look. Why don't you call me when you know what you're going to do." And sure, the brass agreed.

The final negotiations—the deal in which NBC tried to match or better CBS's offer—took place during the Christmas holiday. At this point Jay's neck was really in the noose and the noose was tightening. And it didn't help matters any that it was Christmas.

Leno: "The whole of NBC and everybody went skiing for two weeks. They all went on vacation, and I'm sitting home. You know, trying to call people. 'Can you—well, try the north slope. Will you see if he's there? All right, thank you.' We just kind of sat here and did our shows, and when they came back, they still didn't have a decision, and then we finally found out on a Thursday."

David Letterman did walk at the end of these protracted and complicated negotiations. He walked largely at the urging of his own powerful agent, Michael Ovitz. He walked, in addition, because he did not like the long gap between then and the night he would be taking over *The Tonight Show.* He walked because he was still plenty miffed at the way the NBC brass had treated him in the long haul.

The day he announced he was moving to CBS at a big press conference, there was an earlier press conference held by the NBC brass for Jay Leno. Number One Point: Jay Leno was staying on *The Tonight Show.* Number Two Point: David Letterman was moving from NBC to CBS to start a new late-night show when his contract with NBC ran out in August 1993.

Jay was relieved when he heard the news. And yet NBC had hedged and ducked and bobbed all over the place, playing some kind of weird game with him, much as they had hedged and ducked and bobbed playing a game with David Letterman. The star of *The Tonight Show* had every reason to be miffed—perhaps even more miffed than David Letterman.

Yet true to his style, Leno came out swinging in a kind of upbeat, in-your-face attitude. In effect, he made light of the whole thing. He appeared suddenly and loudly at the press conference in

Burbank on one of his favorite motorbikes, pop-popping as he came scorching up to the microphones. Then he hopped off, allowing Warren Littlefield to say the words that were the key to the press conference: "The host of *The Tonight Show* will continue to be Mr. Jay Leno!"

Then Leno grinned and got off a choice barb at the NBC brass, which had finally stopped playing games with him.

"Don't let those NBC guys out of your sights." He grinned, did a little body English, and went to his punch line. "Welcome to NBC, which stands for 'Never Believe your Contract.' "

Leno went on. "It's a great soap opera. It's the kind of thing people like to read about. Essentially, you have millionaires arguing. And no matter who loses, everybody winds up rich and whatever. And you get egg on your face. This was not a case of two people auditioning for the job and somebody got it. I mean, I *had* the job."

Then, looking puzzled a moment, Leno continued. "What we're celebrating is the fact that I *haven't* been fired." He gave the camera a *Twilight Zone* look. "Very strange."

When he was asked by a reporter if he felt hurt by the ongoing controversy, Leno said: "Everybody was honorable. A little indecisive," he added, grinning as he let the comment hang there without further elucidation.

After this brouhaha the late-night scene settled down to a more sedate rhythm, with Letterman doing his 12:30 stint with his usual flair—he would be starting at CBS with his new show in August 1993—and Leno doing his new 11:35 stint with far greater care than he had before. He now had a staff of a dozen-odd writers, and other free-lancers who faxed in gags whenever they seemed appropriate. In spite of the harried pace at which his nightly show proceeded, Leno *still* honed many of his gags at popular comedy clubs.

Frank Swertlow caught one of Leno's appearances at the Comedy & Magic Club at Hermosa Beach for a *TV Guide* story in August 1993. Accompanying Leno was Jimmy Brogan, one of *The Tonight Show* writers and a right-hand man for Leno. It was Brogan's job to work each night with Leno and another writer, Chuck Martin, to put together a selection of the night's gags from a choice of about two hundred originals.

But Leno's stint at the Comedy & Magic Club was an additional honing.

There was, of course, a Dan Quayle joke. "Did you see in the paper that Dan Quayle is working at the Hudson Institute?" Leno asked. "This is a think tank in Indiana. Quayle working at a think tank . . . let's hope there's a lifeguard on duty." Big laugh.

Then Leno turned to Clinton for a twit or two. "I love this revisionist history," Leno said. "They always say while in college they may have experimented with drugs—like in the basement of the frat house with a Bunsen burner. 'Hey, Bill, want to come to the beer blast?' 'No, we have to finish these marijuana experiments.'" More laughs.

And, of course there was the topical gag about Bosnia. "Now we are dropping food," Leno noted. "There hasn't been this much food thrown out of an airplane since Continental Airlines introduced chicken à la king to their menu." Another big laugh.

Then Leno went after McDonald's, which had just announced they would accept credit cards for meals. Leno: "Miss a couple of payments on your cheeseburger and they put a McLien on your house."

Leno to Swetlow: "Comedy is like a muscle; if you don't use it, it begins to atrophy."

Later that night, at Leno's house in Beverly Hills, Leno assembled Brogan and Martin to go over the jokes for the night's standup.

Leno, reading aloud: "Famed author Scott Turow has a new legal thriller, about a lawyer who disappears from sight. So it has a happy ending."

Silence.

Leno: "Anybody like that?"

Brogan shook his head. "A little simplistic."

"A little overdone," Martin said.

The next joke revolved around marriage. Nobody liked it. "I don't put down marriage on the show," Leno explained. "It makes it sound like I have trouble at home."

In the end, hours later, the kitchen cabinet had winnowed out about two dozen jokes, which were read into the tape recorder for Monday night's standup.

By the time a year had elapsed from the night Jay Leno took over for Johnny Carson, the viewing audience for *The Tonight Show* had dropped by about 6 percent. For the year between May 1992 and May 1993 he was seen in an average of about 4.2 million homes a night, compared to 3 million for Rush Limbaugh, 2.7 million for Arsenio Hall, and 2.4 million for David Letterman. ABC's politically oriented news program *Nightline* averaged about 4.5 million homes a night, somewhat ahead of Leno's show.

Even if the ratings for *The Tonight Show* had gone down somewhat compared to the last two years of Johnny Carson's regime, the show had retained its ranking as television's most popular late-night entertainment program.

Nevertheless, Leno became more and more uneasy as the months rolled by. A newspaper story reported a conversation overheard between NBC Entertainment President Warren Littlefield and a veteran performer. The performer asked the question, "Why is Jay doing bad?"

Littlefield was quick to respond. "What are you saying? He's pulled in a younger demographic, his ratings are holding their own. We're very happy with Jay."

And the questioner nodded sagely. "Oh, so then it's true. He *is* doing bad."

The performer knew the game. When the higher-ups professed that they were "happy" about anything it meant that they were *not*—and that something was wrong.

There were other little clues to the disenchantment, too. Someone showed Leno a cartoon by Henry Martin from *The New Yorker* magazine. It showed a burly, roustabout type dressed in a suit jacket and an open-necked shirt seated in the first-chair position of a talk show. "If this will help your ratings, Jay, I think your listeners would be interested to learn that while I was breaking into show business I constructed an A-bomb, which I dismantled after I got my first major part."

It was a double-edged caption. Was it simply an indication of the kind of guests Jay Leno had? Or did it mean that he would do *anything* for better ratings, including the use of threats and assaults of terrorists? Pretty dark humor, in any case there.

And so Jay Leno did his own research on the show, examining it as mercilessly as he could, trying to see if it was on the good side or on the bad side of that invisible median set up by the public. According to the ratings, the monologue at the beginning was always the part of the show to score highest. When he had started out in May 1992, the monologues usually ran about four and a half minutes. By the end of the year, they were running seven or eight minutes—sometimes as long as ten minutes.

The key to the question was that people always told him they liked the monologues the best. What was more, most of the jokes about Washington and the Democrats and Republicans had a good cutting edge to them. As far as Leno was concerned, they were better subjects for humor than homosexuals and the type of material other comics did.

However, one critic of the show noted that there was what he called "a chain-link rhythm of setup and punch, setup and punch," which was repeated every night. Also, the jokes were frequently recycled—about Clinton, Ted Kennedy, Bob Dole, Dan Quayle, and so on. And the critic didn't like the fact that Leno *still* tended to snicker like a kid at his jokes, particularly those that didn't come off.

As for the interviews, they were still the softest things Leno did. But he felt he had been doing better with them. What bothered him when he ran the tapes of his shows was the fact that he made no attempt to hide the notes he held in his hands as he asked his questions. He then made an effort to abandon the notes and to keep the questions in his mind from memory.

He was also guilty of what are called softball—or very easy—questions asked of certain celebrities. Leno continued to deal in softball questions, although he occasionally tried to put a harder, more cutting edge to them.

He noted a tendency in himself at the time to muddy up his jokes and questions with excess verbiage that could cover up and dampen the possibility of a laugh that might erupt into something bigger. "The new edition of *Webster's Dictionary* really reflects our evolving language," he said one night. "I looked up 'tax cut' and it said, 'See tax hike.' "

Now that's the joke. And yet, suddenly fearful that there might not be a laugh at all, or even a snicker, Leno picked up with explanatory verbiage, something like: "So it really does reflect what's going on in the country." Or words to that effect.

When Leno had selected Branford Marsalis as musical director of *The Tonight Show,* he had taken a giant step in the direction of affirmative action and had been cautiously but roundly cheered for his daring. However, once the band was in place, there were murmurs from people who were used to Doc Severinsen's bunch—and who wondered what was going on with this *new* bunch.

Marsalis and Leno were more out of synch than ever with each other—that was obvious. When Leno turned to Marsalis during some lull in the jokes in order to get a quick fix, it was supposed to work out into a laugh of some kind that would bring the show back on track.

But generally the mike in Marsalis's hand was cold. It had always tended to be that way. Marsalis was a musician, not a talker. Nevertheless, Leno was hopeful and felt that things would work out for the better. At first he had received a number of letters from fans. "We don't understand what the band's doing." And then, after a few months of watching the band, it turned out that the viewers rather liked the new band because they had changed over to what the viewers wanted.

The band had changed nothing!

Maybe the same thing would happen with Marsalis. Maybe.

Leno was aware that he had always been perceived as a host who was "too nice" to his guests. It wasn't that he was nice, exactly. It was simply that he had always believed in treating other people with the respect they deserved. He operated from an old show biz rule of thumb: If you *don't* treat people with respect, they won't mind going down as long as they can bring you down with them.

Even in the darkest days during the Letterman crisis, Jay Leno had felt the loyalty and support of a number of people in the hierarchy of NBC. What made it right for Leno was the fact that those who were loyal to him did not lie to him, as they could easily have done. "Oh, you're in, baby! We love you!" Of course the affair could have been handled quite differently. But the fact was, he did have loyal supporters, and he was not being lied to constantly.

Even the Letterman fiasco—when it was obvious that NBC had simply ignored the presence of Jay Leno and offered *The Tonight Show* to David Letterman, after Leno was under contract and had begun hosting the show—had not turned him completely against the network. After all, the Letterman crisis was a typical show business syndrome. It was something that had to be endured—a difficult thing when it was obvious that it was quite possible that Jay Leno was going to lose *The Tonight Show* before the crisis was finally neutralized.

In examining the fiasco with Helen Kushnick, Leno realized that he had taken some bad advice from people on certain things. He was learning as best he could how to handle advice. The booking problem almost broke the back of *The Tonight Show*. He knew that he would never allow that to happen again.

Letterman was taken on by CBS at a salary of $14 million a year. Leno's contract was something like $3 million. However, as a result of Letterman's departure, Leno was able to get more money for everyone on the show. And he had a contract with another two years to go.

Now Letterman was out there and about to become a stiff competitor to Jay Leno. Leno knew it would be a rough battle. And he had no idea who was going to win. He felt that both shows would probably share about equally at least for the first couple of years. But after that, it was anybody's ball game.

It all depended on how Letterman's brand of wit would go down with an audience that was used to different fare at 11:35 P.M. than at 12:30 A.M.

That was all in the future. As for now, however, Leno had won one of the skirmishes. As he told Al Roker on the *Today Show,* "They literally said to me, 'You'll either be fired or you'll be our hope for the year 2000.' So, you're either fired, or you're the future of television in late night!"

There was no doubt about which alternative Leno would hold out for.

Ringing in the Changes I

From the moment the curtain rose on David Letterman's CBS debut on August 30, 1993, it was obvious that a great deal of blood, sweat, and tears had gone into the transition from NBC's *Late Night with David Letterman* to the brand-new *Late Show with David Letterman* on CBS. What was more, the work had obviously paid off. The moment the full view of the set with Letterman smiling at the audience was on screen, viewers the world over knew that this one was going to be a solid hit.

The set itself was a masterpiece. CBS had purchased the old Ed Sullivan Building on Broadway, where the famous *Ed Sullivan Show*s of the nineteen -forties, -fifties, and -sixties had originated—including the Beatles' U.S. debut in 1964—and had brought it up to date with a set showing Broadway behind the host's desk, along with a hauntingly beautiful skyline of New York City. Although the scene was an obvious reworking of the old-style Johnny Carson *Tonight* set, the details were done with flair and style.

The audience was seated in comfortable seats ascending to the rear in traditional amphitheatrical fashion, with plenty of room between the desk and the audience for Letterman to perform whatever bits of intellectual legerdemain he wanted without encumbrance. There was a feeling of comfort and assurance to the stage and the set. CBS had accomplished exactly what it had set out to do.

But the big change was in the appearance of Letterman himself. Here was no aging hippie trapped in a time warp about to deliver odes to pot and boring homilies for world peace—the image Letterman's detractors loved to project in the public mind. Here was a tall, gracious man, urbane and friendly, dressed stylishly in a trim dark suit, with a neat and beautifully designed tie, shined shoes, and looking every inch the debonaire New York patrician.

He sailed into his stand-up routine, smiling and thanking the management of CBS for the tasteful, low-key promotion preceding his debut—an obvious ironic reference to the mind-boggling blitz that had been engineered by the CBS paper brigade. The argument about "intellectual properties" came up again, with Letterman pointing out that he had checked NBC's attorneys and found that yes, he could use the name Dave even on his new network.

Tom Brokaw, NBC's news anchorman, appeared to wish him "reasonably well." He wandered over to the cue cards and riffled through them. "I'm a little shocked. Dave, I'm *disappointed.*" He grabbed up two cards. "These two jokes are the intellectual property of NBC!" And he walked off the set.

After another joke or two Letterman introduced Paul Newman, seated in the audience. Newman stood up, acknowledging the applause, and then said: "Where the hell are the singing cats?" When Letterman told him the musical *Cats* was just down the street, Newman frowned. "I'm in the wrong theater!" And he too walked out.

Comedian Bill Murray was his initial guest—reprising Murray's appearance on David Letterman's first late-night show for NBC ten years before. He became involved in spray-painting DAVE on the host's desk. The sprayer jammed but Murray finally got the job done anyway.

He then explained that there were a lot of people who did not know who Dave was, and he wanted to help Dave out so he would be recognized more.

There followed a filmed sequence with Letterman in the field chatting with people at their front doors and on the sidewalks— one of the most successful of his show's comic elements. And, of course, there was a Top Ten List.

All in all, Dave's opener was a humdinger. He did exactly what he had to do to move from his time-warp spot of 12:30 A.M. to the more civilized 11:35 P.M. spot. And he had reinvented himself completely, shedding all his freakish intellectual baggage for a more cosmopolitan image.

The proof of the pudding was in the Nielsens. Within a month of Letterman's debut on CBS, he was named the new "King of Late Night" by *USA Today* writer Jefferson Graham. Not only was he winning the ratings race itself, but he was also grabbing on to the hard-to-get younger viewers that all the advertisers were drooling about.

Television-watching during the late-night hours (including 11:35) was up about 10 percent, thanks to the debut of the Letterman show. His ratings outstripped Jay Leno's—whose average was running almost the same as it had before Letterman's appearance.

Letterman's average was about a solid 5 rating, twice as high as Letterman's old rating at 12:30. It was stronger than Johnny Carson had been pulling in his last *Tonight Show* years. He usually rated somewhere in the mid 4 numbers—translating out to about 3,768,000 television households.

It had been hoped by NBC that *The Tonight Show,* carried by 99 percent of the NBC affiliates, would handily win the ratings race for at least a year after Letterman's move to CBS, because CBS was handicapped by the fact that 30 percent of their affiliates delayed Letterman until midnight or 12:30. Factoring in that 30 percent handicap would give CBS another rating point, or 4,710,000 potential television households. In fact, Letterman's ratings were actually better than they *seemed,* and they seemed very good indeed.

"David is hot and trendy," one observer noted. "Watching Dave is the hip thing to do right now. Our research tells us that people like to talk to others about what they watched on TV the night before. They like shared viewing experiences, and that's what makes shows like *Seinfeld* and *60 Minutes* so popular. Letterman gives people something to talk about."

Amazingly enough, the ratings war between Leno and Letterman actually brought many more viewers into the time period. "I don't think everybody expected [Letterman] to do as strong as he did," another observer said. "But what we have found, the majority of his viewing audience didn't come from the other talk shows. He has brought new viewers into the time period."

The ratings battle generally followed the booking patterns of the two shows. For example, during his second week on CBS, Letterman's ratings zoomed one night when he had Vice President Al Gore on. The following week, Leno beat him one night when he had on Burt Reynolds, who discussed his breakup with Loni

Anderson. And, of course, *Nightline*'s overnight ratings went through the roof when President Clinton appeared on the show.

The consensus was that in the Leno-Letterman battle, "Letterman will have a younger audience, and *The Tonight Show* will have an older audience who will stick with Leno, although he will pick up the younger viewers on nights when he has the hot guest. But it's hard to say who will end up in first."

It was all well and good for prognosticators to try to read the future, but it did little good for Jay Leno, the man who was most concerned over how the future would work out for him. The days after the Letterman show started on CBS were the darkest days of his life. The three or four weeks after Letterman's opening show were a black hole.

"That was when it was fun for people to get on the bandwagon and take shots at me." Jay's critics in the press wrote him down day after day. Even his friends and associates—other comedians!—ganged up on him. There was talk about how he was slipping—doomsday stuff that showed him on a quick trip to oblivion. The executives who had stood by him all the way through the debacle of the Letterman situation now began to make snide remarks about Leno's talents and abilities. Some of the higher-ups even admitted that NBC had made one of the greatest blunders in corporate television history by selecting Leno over Letterman.

Well-wishers sidled up to him. Do this. Do that. Try this out. Are you sure this is working? Why don't you try something *new*?

He had been there before, not in exactly the same situation, but in similar ones. And he had always worked himself free. Could he do it again? Now he didn't know. He had waged an exhausting war against the threat of Letterman in gearing up *The Tonight Show* after the Helen Kushnick debacle. Apparently he had not done enough.

*   *   *

In May 1994, the people around David Letterman decided to make a quick sortie out of New York for greener pastures—namely L.A. The bookings would be easier there. The talent was free for the taking. And a change of venue was always good for a freshly blossoming, really blooming show. And the Letterman show was a big success—not only in itself but in relation to its main competition, *The Tonight Show.*

Somehow the hovering presence of Letterman over Leno's shoulder unnerved him. His nemesis would be much too close to him. It was decided that Jay Leno would also seek a change in venue for a week in May. And the plans were made accordingly. Leno felt that even if he did not win the ratings race because of a trip to New York—and nothing hinted at the fact that he even *might*—he'd take the trip anyway. He was a road guy to begin with. Maybe a return to the road would change his luck.

NBC cleaned up its rather intimately small studio 8-H from which *Saturday Night Live* was broadcast each week and readied it for *The Tonight Show* gang on its New York tour. Leno made a lot of public appearances on NBC shows—the news crew, the weatherman, the people on *Today*—and helped get his image across to people who did not see him every day. It was more or less a relaxing gig—and Leno decided to take it for just that.

It was his first night on the cramped set of *Saturday Night Live* that viewers who had been pulling for Leno but who did not really know why their comedian had sunk so far in the ratings noticed an odd thing. There was an electricity about Leno's performance that had been missing for some time. He radiated excitement and humor and charisma. What was more, his jokes were funnier. The audience responded ecstatically. It was a smaller audience than usual—but it was boiling with enthusiasm.

Even the interviews went better. With the audience pressed in so close, it seemed that they too were part of the conversations. A rare intimacy gripped the set and it radiated over the airwaves to everyone tuned in across the country. Leno was back in the nightclubs again, where he had first honed the Jay Leno imago. The magic was back. He looked *good.*

In point of fact, Leno had been privately reinventing himself, particularly in regard to his political stance. He had always been good at deflating hypocrites—and where did one find hypocrites more than in popular politics? Leno had taken to heart the criticism that he was "too nice" to everybody, particularly politicians, who should have developed hard skins by the very nature of their business.

Although this particular slant had gone unobserved in Burbank by those who were critiquing him, it became obvious in the more tightly controlled atmosphere of the *Saturday Night Live* studios. And for that reason, his political stuff and his regular jokes came off better, had more zip to them, didn't pull the punches anymore.

Leno returned from New York with a rather formidable agenda in mind. He was down but he was not out. He thought he had discovered weak spots in his own comedic style. He knew how to correct them. And he *would* correct them.

Within days of his return to the West Coast, Leno got in touch with the stage designer of the *Saturday Night Live* set and hired him to build a stylish, up-to-date theater set for *The Tonight Show* in Los Angeles. The main stipulation was that the performing part of the stage should be much closer to the audience than the old *Tonight Show* set. Mary Murphy quoted Leno in a *TV Guide* story in Oc-

tober 1994: "I don't want this stage anymore. This is Johnny's stage.
I want my stage."

And he got it.

When Leno had first taken over the reins of *The Tonight Show*
from Carson, he had not changed much of anything in the decor
and architecture of the set. Carson had always walked onto the
proscenium out of a rainbow-colored curtain at the start of the show.
Leno did the same thing, except he changed the color of the curtain
to shades of gray and blue.

But now there were a lot of changes in the physical surroundings
of the set. The auditorium's color scheme and configuration were
altered radically from the Carson show, whose set had been more
staid and inconspicuous. Leno's designer changed that staidness into
a more vibrant multicolored milieu that Leno felt was a more accurate reflection of the 1990s than the earlier decor.

Bold colors accentuated the setting, with tones like mustard and
cerise highlighting each other in Day-Glo hues as colored spots
illuminated the entire auditorium. Carson's show had favored the
brassy look of the Big Band Era of the late thirties; Leno's favored
a more flamboyant echo of the early rock era—after all, he was of
the boomer generation, too!—but without the need for the electronic amplification favored by the rockers.

Even the show's opening took on a new look. No longer does
Leno walk out from behind a curtain. Now there is a taped montage
of scenes à la *Saturday Night Live* to dazzle the TV viewer. Then
the camera cuts to Leno, who is already out to stand on his spot,
or walking toward it, preparing to regale the crowd with one-liners.

However, before commencing the monologue, Leno now

shakes hands with members of the audience closest to him in the front rows—like a charismatic politician on the hustings scenting the aroma of victory in the air. Rocking from side to side onstage, hammering his fists sporadically, Leno then launches into his monologue, trying to work up the audience with his gags, or with his body English if for some reason the joke lines fail.

Leno has also made spectacular changes in the monologue itself—changes that have nothing to do with the words he speaks, but in the "fringe benefits." For example, filmed gags and even news footage might be interspliced with the monologue material—such as a bungee jumper falling flat on his face in *The Tonight Show* parking lot, or whatever. The splash and color of the film clips add a great deal of technological pizzazz to the monologue without taking away from it. Never had Carson dared do anything to divert attention from his monologue.

Even Leno would never have used such high-tech stuff in his early years on *The Tonight Show.* Nor would he have dreamed of using cutting-edge technological gimmicks in his act. But when he remade the show, he threw out all the rules and opened the gates to any kind of technical enhancement available—all in aid of making the audience laugh. And indeed the audiences did approve, as they slowly at first and then rapidly began to desert David Letterman and tuned back in to Jay Leno to see how far he would push the envelope in the direction of high-tech show-biz pizzazz.

Like Carson, Jay Leno continues to invent recurring routines that sometimes feature audience participation as well, sometimes, as simply featured taped gags for quick showing. Whereas Carson had "Stump the Band," in which he walked into the audience and asked members to sing a song that the Doc Severinsen Band had never heard. Leno came up with "Midnight Confessions," in which he steps into the audience and, with the falsetto preachy voice of a televangelist, coaxes members to confess some egregious sin they have committed. After they do so, a slight character named Gilbert, clad all in black, sprints into the audience and chastises the sinner.

For example, a teenage girl admitted to dancing nude on a table. After she finished, Gilbert whisked over to her from the side of the auditorium and screamed in her face, "You cheap slut!"

And Leno continually invents new, recurring characters, such as Iron Jay (Jay's own head morphed into a larger size), Mr. Brain (another morphing of Jay's head), Beyondo (Jay's detached head with white wig and beard floating about the set), Evil Jay (another concoction of Jay), and others, including Billy Tuttle, Jay Katz (Jay's cat), and Larry the Lawyer.

Even so, the characters are simply the conduit from the show to the viewer—it is always the *jokes* that count for the most with the audience.

Jay Leno was also moving in another new direction. It became apparent that he was wearing his hair just a shade longer than he had been throughout his first months as *Tonight Show* host. He also began to dress down deliberately, occasionally showing up without a tie on. And he began to wear more casual attire.

Mary Murphy quoted Leno further: "I don't want to wear ties anymore. Johnny wore ties. I don't want to wear ties unless I feel like wearing them. I don't want to dress like Johnny. I don't want to do this like Johnny. This is my show."

Although at first the changes were imperceptible except to the very attentive, his material had a much sharper edge to it. The gags came out more quickly and surely—not slowly and guardedly as formerly. And yet he did not in any way alter any of his previous precepts about comedic material.

Rick Ludwin, NBC's senior vice president of late night, and Gary Considine, NBC Productions executive vice president, were the execs responsible for the remodeling of *The Tonight Show* set to enhance Leno's strengths.

Ludwin explained: "Jay's the first to admit that he wasn't experienced enough in day-to-day television production to know what it was that had been missing in the old studio. The minute that he got to New York and felt that energy and that proximity to the audience, he knew what was missing and what he needed to fertilize the show here."

Leno agreed. "Oh yeah, I'm a lot more comfortable on the new set. You need to do things your own way, and my way has always been to have the audience as close as physically possible. That's what it's like in the nightclubs, and it seems to bring the audience in tight, seeing their faces and playing off their reactions. I enjoy the interplay and really thrive on it."

In fact, he was doing his own preshow warm-ups only a yard away from the first row of seats in the audience.

Another important change in the show's format was Leno's handling of his monologue. Ever since taking over at *Tonight*, he had been extending his monologue from the usual four or five minutes to seven to ten minutes, and occasionally even to a quarter of an hour. He would then do live or pretaped sketches with other actors or perhaps a comedy bit by himself—all for insertion during the monologue.

He pointed out, "I think these shows have ceased to be talk

shows and are comedy-variety shows. With the sketches and the monologues today, I am trying to do less of the one-liners and do jokes with more of an attitude."

He still does not wield his political humor in order to change his audience's political views. "The thing I always say about political humor is, you don't change anybody's mind, you just reinforce what they already believe. So you wield power, yeah, if that means you have an audience. But if you ever go against the audience's grain, then, of course, you don't have any power."

Leno feels he must exercise caution in his choice of material for jokes so that he will not offend anyone. "You tell a joke about the pope, for example—like when he was in Denver—you have to be careful. People hear 'the pope,' and they think, like, 'What did he say when he made fun of the pope?'"

A good, safe joke for Leno is one about his own childhood.

"To me, one of the funny things about life is how you can grow into the kind of person that you used to think was just the worst. Years ago, when I was a mechanic and I would go visit people who had a lot of fancy cars, I would automatically assume—even if they were self-made types—that they didn't know anything about their cars and really didn't deserve to have them. And now here I am with all my cars."

Here's another example of one of Leno's rather gentle anecdotes about his boyhood in Massachusetts—but it says a lot about Leno's perception of the work ethic:

"I got to Boston on a Sunday, saw this car place, and said to myself, 'Oh, I'll get a job there.' So on Monday I went in and asked for a job. The boss said they didn't need anybody. The next day I came back and I said to the foreman, 'Hi, I'm the new wash guy.'

"And he said, 'Oh, okay,' and he told me what to do.

"I washed cars for two or three days before the boss asked me what I was doing.

" 'I'm washing,' I said.

" 'Oh, who hired you?'

" 'Well,' I said, 'I just came in and figured, you know, I'd just work for free until you needed me or something.'

"So he asked the foreman how I was doing, and the foreman said, 'Okay.'

" 'All right,' he said to me, 'you're hired.' "

The important thing for Leno was not to become another Mort Sahl, even though he himself was an ardent fan of Sahl. The problem with Sahl, according to Leno, was that he went overboard with his political humor.

"I remember what happened when he tried to tell people about Jim Garrison and his theories about the Kennedy assassination. They just lost interest and turned away. I went to see him in Boston once at a small club. It was packed. And he came up with the charts and graphs, and by the end of his two hours, only thirty of us were left."

For Leno, "the real trick is joke first, then deliver any sort of underlying message second. Believe me, if there's something in there, people will find it."

Leno has always had a concept of good political humor. Re Teddy Kennedy: "If no other contenders emerge, Kennedy could have the nomination in his pocket. Now if he could just find his pants, that would be great."

Leno maintains that joke always gets a big laugh. "So much bigger than the joke really warrants."

As Neal Karlen, a correspondent, put it, "Leno refuses to lecture like Lenny Bruce, pontificate like Mort Sahl, or cop false anger like Eddie Murphy."

The upshot? Jokes like:

"My wife loves Europe, but to me it's a bad day at a theme park."

Or the one about Jerry Brown, a.k.a. Governor Moonbeam of California, when he ran for president. "Jerry Brown's been working pretty good. The sad thing about the Brown candidacy is that all the people who want to vote for him are locked inside that Biosphere II experiment."

Or: "I read that Nancy Reagan was at the Beverly Hills Hotel to accept her Humanitarian of the Year Award. I'm glad she beat out that conniving bitch Mother Teresa."

Or did you hear the one about Prescott Bush? "Here's one I was going to try about Prescott Bush. You know, [the former] president's brother. You're aware they say he's involved with the Japanese Mafia. He says he didn't know why, but he woke up one morning and found the front end of a Toyota in his bed."

The ratings war between Leno and Letterman continued on its uneven course. Letterman was still ahead in the long run, but occasionally a special night would put Leno right up there tying him. And once in a while, he actually *beat* Letterman. But the week-by-week averages all went to Letterman.

Then came the O. J. Simpson trial. And, in a couple of ways, it gave *The Tonight Show* a leg up. Even during the preliminary hearings in 1994, Leno was right on top of the trial and the interesting people involved in the case. About Marcia Clark, the chief prosecutor, Leno said:

"She's tough. She's really tough. Do you know what her nickname was in college? Hillary."

When the trial started, Leno began to get a lot of mileage out of it. One night during his warm-up, he stood with his hands crossed behind his back, wiggling his fingers. "What's this?" he asked the audience, referring to his odd posture. Answer: "O.J. signing autographs."

The most memorable treasures from the O. J. Simpson trial on *The Tonight Show* were the Dancing Itos, a group of terpsichoreans who showed up every few nights to do comedy bits based on the trial and what had happened in court that day.

Judge Lance Ito, who presided over the double murder trial, never complained about Leno's sketches featuring the Dancing Itos. These were five young Asian-Americans, gotten up like Judge Ito, wearing spectacles and false beards, and hoofing their way across *The Tonight Show* stage, their black robes flaring about their legs. They first appeared on the show March 2, 1995.

Larry King once asked Leno how he had managed to get such perfect dancers for the rather risky comic dancing effect of multiple Judge Itos.

"We just put in a call for Asian-American dancers," Leno told him. "And we used what we got. It worked out very well." There was no real agenda that the show was after—just good clean fun and a laugh or two.

The audience couldn't get enough of the wacky act. Hundreds of letters poured into *Tonight*'s Burbank studio, demanding a return engagement of the dance troupe. Heeding his fans, Leno kept inviting them back.

The inspirational addition of a look-alike for Assistant District Attorney Marcia Clark enhanced the audience's delight and kept them screaming for more. The Clark look-alike would appear in black fishnet stockings and perform a Vegas-style cancan while the Dancing Itos sang "O.J.L.A.," a spoof on the Village People's song, "Y.M.C.A."

Not only did Judge Ito refrain from complaining about the kooky act, he loved it.

Leno claims that one reason the Dancing Itos were funny was because of the name Ito. "The name Ito is fun to say. It's like Buttafuoco."

The advantage of Leno's continual featuring of the O. J. Simpson trial in his stand-up jokes was the fact that Letterman refused to do anything about the trial at first, claiming, quite sincerely, that it was improper to do so on a comedy show. The murders were not funny; nor was the spectacle of a trial particularly amusing. In the end, however, even Letterman began doing jokes about the trial.

Leno once outlined his reasons for focusing on the Simpson trial. "On *The Tonight Show,* our humor is not based on the murders themselves," he explained. "We mostly stay away from references about O.J. and Nicole and Ronald Goldman. We attempt to deal with the media hype, the strange things that are happening in the trial and all the colorful chracters."

A typical gag might be: "Did you see that today [at the O. J. Simpson trial]? Did you see while testifying, Kato ran his hands through his hair and O.J.'s knife fell out!"

Leno: "The characters are fascinating. You've got Kato Kaelin, who's kind of like everybody's brother-in-law. To many, he's the epitome of what life out here [in California] is all about. To some degree, the trial deals with the antics of the rich and beautiful.

"I think the monologues and skits provide viewers an escape from the serious aspects of the trial. There's a sense of the ridiculous . . . that appeals to many people. That's what we're concentrating on—not the blood and gore surrounding the murder."

Leno noted: "I've tried to keep a sense of balance. My jokes always imply O.J.'s guilty, but we also did a lot of jokes about Mark Fuhrman and the planting of evidence. I did a lot of Johnnie Cochran jokes, but I also spent a lot of time defending him. . . . That gave both sides a chance to laugh, and when I look out and see a racially mixed crowd laughing at the same joke, I think I've done my job."

In the end Leno had a comment of his own about the trial. "Los Angeles is spending two million dollars a month on this trial. And people in Washington are talking about cutting out school lunch programs? There's something out of whack here."

When the trial was over and charges against Simpson were dismissed by the jury, Leno continued ribbing Simpson. After O. J. Simpson had held a number of lengthy telephone interviews on national television and radio, Leno began getting telephone calls on the set during his show from "O. J. Simpson," too, purportedly asking Leno to buy his video, and so on.

There were plenty of other subjects to intrigue Leno besides the Simpson trial. He turned the John Wayne Bobbitt affair against the network itself: "The network was pushing me to have him do a walk-on here . . . because it would be good for the ratings. To me, Bobbitt is a wife-beater. Why reward somebody like that by putting him on TV? That's not entertainment, that's sensationalism."

He was annoyed at Dennis Miller, the comedian, who blamed Leno for the booking wars in 1992 that had ended in Helen Kushnick's departure from *The Tonight Show*. "I went on Larry King and said I had called him up and invited him on *The Tonight Show,* and the next day he said I was a liar. Of course I said it. Do I think he is talented? Yes. I do find it odd that people seem to forget who got him his apartment when he came out here . . . who lent money to his brother to buy a car."

In the fall of 1995, Leno was talking about an upcoming reunion special of *Cagney & Lacy,* starring Tyne Daly and Sharon Gless. As he went on talking about the stars, he described the show itself as "pound for pound, the best TV movie on." Wha' happened to Mr. Nice Guy?

It was during the summer of 1995 that Leno really made inroads not only in the ratings, but in the number of viewers who had never watched him before. He had Hugh Grant on shortly after the English actor was arrested for propositioning a prostitute in Hollywood.

Leno: "Let me start with question number one: What the hell were you thinking?"

Grant: "It's not easy. The thing is, people have given me tons of ideas on this one. I keep reading new psychological theories and stuff like that: 'I was under pressure. I was tired. I was lonely. I fell down the stairs when I was a child.' But I think it would be bollocks to hide behind something like that. I think you know in life what's a good thing to do and what's a bad thing. I did a bad thing, and there you have it."

If he were not the subject of the story, Grant admitted that he would "be enjoying it as much as anyone else. But it's pretty miserable on the other side of the equation. In a way, I need to suffer for this. . . . I completely understand everyone having a good joke about it. But it's bad when they are jostling your father. . . . I called him and that was a bad phone call to make. He just said, 'Well, look, old boy, I was in the army and I know that sort of thing.' Cool, really cool."

Outside *The Tonight Show* studio a woman stood holding up a large sign that read quite plainly: "I Would Have Paid You, HUGH."

This booking coup was no brainy star's foresight, no race to see who could grab Grant the fastest after his arrest. The ironic thing was that the actor had already been signed on to flog a movie he was in—*Nine Months*—when he was arrested on June 27!

Whatever, Leno struck pure gold with the interview. For the first time in almost two years of head-to-head competition—ninety weeks in all—*The Tonight Show*'s weekly average moved ahead of *The Late Show with David Letterman*. What was more, newcomers to the show continued to tune in night after night, so that the ratings seesaw was more balanced then ever, with Leno's end very nicely up.

Admitting to *People* magazine in December 1995 that he had indeed been "overreverential" to people in the past, he said that he had moved on beyond that spot now. "I can tell Schwarzenegger, 'Arnold, you're getting a gut!' And he'll grab my head and say, 'Jay, you little wimp!' "

It was a significant breakthrough—*The Tonight Show* trouncing the "King of Late Night TV," *The Late Show with David Letterman*. Was it simply an aberration? Or would the numbers last in favor of Leno?

Ringing in the Changes II

By the year 1994, Jay Leno had become aware of a situation in the show that must be remedied. Not all the members of his vast audience were thoroughly enamored of the musical background provided by Branford Marsalis. Although Leno had been able to persuade Marsalis to eschew some of his classic jazz style in favor of a more popular musical approach, he could not get him to relax while he was on camera.

Marsalis had his backers, too—backers who wanted an even more traditional jazz treatment than Marsalis had been giving. In October 1994 *Down Beat* magazine ran an editorial entitled, "We Was Robbed." Starting out with the early Marsalis selections on *The Tonight Show,* the magazine wrote: "Joe Henderson blazed Billy Strayhorn's 'Lush Life' to a wildly appreciative audience. Others followed. Musicians such as Geri Allen, Bobby Watson, Clark Terry, John Scofield, Roy Hargrove, and Everett Harp sat in with the band."

Then—suddenly—it all changed. As Letterman's show began trouncing Leno's in the ratings, the decision was made at *The Tonight Show* to cut back on the band's jazz segments. The show even curtailed the number of jazz artists who regularly appeared on it. Sit-in musical guests were eventually cut down to a few in number.

Marsalis expressed his disagreement with the show's new policy, letting Leno know he felt baffled, and refused to countenance the changes. Marsalis's dissatisfaction rocked *The Tonight Show* host, as had Leno's poor ratings against Letterman.

Jay Leno had nothing against Marsalis. It was the NBC honchos who had demanded that Leno alter the show to improve its sinking status.

As late as July 1992, Marsalis was enjoying his *Tonight Show* gig. Or at least he said so. "It's fun. First of all, we get to play tunes we'd never play on our own gigs. We have a lot of laughs . . . and we've got more exposure than any house band in television history."

By the end of 1994, frustration supplanted the fun. It was only a matter of time before Leno and Marsalis would part company.

As *Down Beat* had it in that same editorial: "Jazz has been virtually weeded out of the band's repertoire, the band's air time reduced. . . . Marsalis has stated his frustration as well as his reluctant resignation to the new ground rules."

In November 1994, Marsalis announced that he was taking a leave of absence from *The Tonight Show* in order to promote an upcoming album of his. He was only halfway through his five-year contract. Coincidentally, he was quoted in the music magazine *BAM* as calling his *Tonight* gig "not my idea of wonderful musical creativity." A late-night source was quoted as calling Marsalis's comments his "farewell address" to *The Tonight Show*.

Marsalis left the show in January 1995 and did not return. By April 1995, Kevin Eubanks, the jazz guitarist of Marsalis's band, became his replacement as leader of the band. He was also asked to handle some work with Jay Leno.

It was noted by most viewers that Kevin's routines with Jay Leno—mostly comedy stuff—had gotten off to a good start from the beginning.

"Jay and I seem to have a natural kind of thing," Kevin said. "I really dig comedy and comedians."

Kevin Eubanks had been a member of Branford Marsalis's *Tonight Show* band from the opening night. Although his first instrument was a violin, at the age of seven he switched to guitar, which he made his own. His mother was a musician who taught kids how to play the piano. A lot of her musical know-how rubbed off on him.

There was no scandal about Marsalis's departure in 1995 from *The Tonight Show*—but there was a story that appeared in the *Indianapolis Star* concerning Marsalis. In effect, Marsalis said that he had been more or less conned into the job as band leader at NBC.

"The job of musical director," he said, "I found out later was just to kiss the ass of the *[Tonight Show]* host, and I ain't no ass kisser. I didn't realize that at the time. I thought we had this rapport, that I would employ a black sensibility."

Marsalis noted that he thought he would be allowed to have an attitude on the show. Yet it seemed to work out all wrong. "When he [Leno] would tell a joke and it bombed, I'd be like, 'Hey. Don't look over here, man. That shit bombed.' " But the public misinterpreted that attitude. They thought Marsalis was disdainful, not just angry. "Then it became, 'Oh, he's surly. He hates his boss.' "

As for Leno, Marsalis conceded that he did indeed "despise" him. "I consider myself an ironist," Marsalis said. "I'm not comfortable playing along with the stereotype games. If to be happy you have to pretend like you're happy, that's not my style. My top lip's so long you can't even see my teeth. What would I look like, trying to give one of those toothy grins, falling off my chair, laughing?"

When push came to shove and the ratings slumped with Letterman's daunting competition opposite *The Tonight Show,* the NBC execs wanted Marsalis to play along with the jokes. Marsalis coolly told them he had not promised to do that when he signed his contract.

"Jay knew that and he supported it. But the people that are really in charge of the show changed their minds."

And so Marsalis left. He formed a new jazz band, a fusion of rock, jazz, reggae, pop, funk, and rap called Buckshot LeFongue.

Meanwhile Kevin Eubanks in his replacement role helped bring some laughs out of the audience in his various routines as second banana to Jay Leno. The mix was successful from the start. Leno never made any public statement about Marsalis's negative assessment of him.

About Kevin Eubanks, Marsalis was always full of praise and compliments. "That job [at *Tonight*] is a job where if you play the game, you can keep it forever. But I've never been a person to play the game. I play my own game. I hired Kevin. I knew he would be great, and I knew he would be my successor, too."

*   *   *

NBC's Entertainment President Warren Littlefield was absolutely right when he told one reporter, "Jay turned the talk show into more of a comedy hour."

Actually, what he had done was cut back drastically on the two weakest features of the show: the interviews and the music. What had been throughout the earlier years of *The Tonight Show* about three-quarters of the program—forty-five minutes of it—was now probably less than half. What had been expanded was the stand-up monologue—sometimes to as long as fifteen to eighteen minutes—to incorporate the comedy bits filmed in advance for use during the show. Now the monologue and the comedy bits were at least half the show, perhaps more.

It was half a comedy-variety show and half a late-night talk show. But it was a lot more exciting, a lot more visually entertaining, and a lot more fun to watch.

The key word was fun.

Leno was always able to come up with occasional good jokes during an interview—an incipient flair that Dick Cavett had spotted even as far back as Leno's first night as regular host of *The Tonight Show*. Tom Cruise, Cavett wrote in a review of the show, was talking about shooting a love scene: "I just lay there naked with my eyes shut."

Leno cut in with a quick one: "That's how some actors get their jobs, but go on."

He was now far more relaxed about putting his quick wit into play during an interview than he had been when he was permanent guest host for Johnny Carson.

As the show mutated into its snappier format, ratings nosed upward. In the middle of 1995, *Tonight* was averaging a 4.6 rating with a 14 share average compared with Letterman's *Late Show* average of a 5.4 rating with a 16 share average. These ratings reflected an increase of 7 percent for Letterman.

The race was even closer in Nielsen's 32 metered markets. From October 3, 1994, to April 9, 1995, *Tonight* pulled in a 5.4/15 average as opposed to *Late Show*'s 5.7/16. Nightly victories were split about fifty-fifty among these metered markets, with *Tonight* acing out *The Late Show* more often than not in Chicago and Los Angeles.

It was a far cry from the pummeling Leno had been taking in the early months of his head-to-head with Letterman.

Howard Rosenberg, the *Los Angeles Times*'s TV critic, offered the following explanation, attributing Leno's success to "a gradual evolution to make over the *Tonight Show* as a much hipper, younger-skewing show":

"I do think Leno is trying to emulate Letterman to a certain extent. It seems to be working. In Jay's case, when a host is on a roll as he is, you can see his self-assurance is coming across to the studio audience and viewers. I have always been a big fan of Letterman's even though he hardly does a monologue and doesn't really try to connect to his audience, so I'm not entirely surprised that Leno is reaching other viewers."

The fact was, Leno wanted so much for his audience to like him that he had developed the habit of shaking hands with first-row members of the audience, trying to establish a bond between comedian and viewers—more or less as if he were just one of the guys, not a multimillionaire Hollywood celebrity.

The *Los Angeles Daily News*'s TV critic Phil Rosenthal disagreed after a fashion:

"I think Jay is coming on stronger [on account of *Tonight*'s makeover], but we can't forget Letterman's clearances on CBS are simply not comparable because of the affiliation switches in some major markets and the network's stumbling in prime time. NBC's stronger performance on Tuesday through Thursday evenings in prime time has given Leno a much stronger lead-in than what he's had in the past. It has also been a big new year for ABC's *Nightline,* but that would mean that it has taken a certain amount of viewers from either of the talk shows."

Debbie Vickers, the executive producer of *The Tonight Show,* claimed that there was a new feeling of harmony on the set because the show's booking practices were better than during the Kushnick regime. No more arm-twisting of celebrities to do *Tonight* before doing *Late Show* or whatever.

Vickers explained, "We do care about bookings, but it is not an obsession. A lot of celebrities—Billy Crystal, Robin Williams, or Arnold Schwarzenegger—will do us first when a movie comes out one year, and the next year they will do Dave [Letterman] first if they have a new movie. We're all very democratic about it. In Helen's [Kushnick's] defense, she was very aggressive and competitive, but you can't be first every time."

Obviously this was not the same *Tonight Show* that Helen Kushnick had run roughshod over.

Leno confessed to being discomfited by Letterman's constant thrashing of him in the ratings—ever since the two shows went head to head with each other in August 1993.

"It was a very uncomfortable situation, with Johnny retiring and Dave leaving NBC to go to CBS at roughly the same time, and having critics say I got [the] job by default. Either way, I was perceived as the bad guy. It feels pretty good not hearing that label attached to me anymore."

His new, improved ratings as of mid-1995 vindicated Leno, as he saw it. "The truth is that Johnny had this incredible record run that will never be repeated, and I'll just be happy if we continue to grow in this competitive environment."

Truth to tell, Leno *wanted* to win the ratings game. He *wanted* it so bad he could taste it. He wanted it so bad he pored over the morning Nielsens, casting around for *Tonight*'s share as well as for that of his rival *Late Show*. After all, this was the Hollywood jungle and nothing could make a celebrity extinct faster than poor ratings.

Leno's recent ratings boost also helped vindicate Rick Ludwin, John Agoglia, and Warren Littlefield for selecting Leno, not Letterman, to succeed Carson. Leno made a point of playing up his ratings hike in May 1995, which redounded to the credit of the three men who had supported him.

"When NBC was supposedly in the toilet and CBS was getting a 60- or 70-share lead-in with the 1994 winter Olympics, we didn't complain. It's just the way it is. Well, people say, 'If it hadn't been for *ER*, you wouldn't have this much of a boost.' This is our third year. *ER* came in September and we're still here. Sure, I'm glad *ER* gives us a 40-share lead-in, and it certainly helps. When our competitors have done well, I haven't been the one to say, 'Well, they're doing well because they have huge lead-ins.' My competitors are doing well because they are doing a good show."

Leno grudgingly admitted he always wanted to defeat Letterman's show in the ratings war, afraid to sound too eager lest it tarnish his nice-guy image.

"I generally like and respect David, because he does an awesome show. I'm not saying we don't want to win, because we do. But we're really just concentrating on producing the best show we can on a day-to-day basis."

One observer simply laid *Tonight*'s success to the shows themselves:

"Leno is the easier watch and Letterman is more uncomfortable
to watch. Letterman has become more cookie-cutter in how the
segments are scheduled, while Leno mixes it up a little more."

In 1994 Bill Carter wrote a tell-all book about the Leno-
Letterman crisis at NBC, titling it *The Late Shift*. It was a very read-
able and successful book, updated in 1995 with additional material
covering what had happened after the book's initial publication.

The cast of characters was large and formidable, including all
the executives and power brokers involved with either Jay Leno or
David Letterman.

Helen Kushnick took umbrage at Bill Carter's book and his
"version of events," as she called it, and sued him for libel soon
after the publication of the book. The case was eventually settled
out of court.

Some time after her dismissal from *The Tonight Show*, Kushnick
moved to New York. She was, according to her longtime Los Angeles attorney Harry Langberg, "hurt by [her dismissal] and she
didn't ever stop being hurt by it, including Leno's treatment of her."

In August 1996 she died of the cancer she had been fighting
for seven years. Jay Leno had no comment on the death of his one-
time manager.

It was inevitable that television, taking a good look at itself
through Bill Carter's bemused eyes, would decide to make some
kind of docudrama about the crises, problems, and manipulations
involved in the attempted solving of the Leno-Letterman fiasco.

HBO finally decided to take the plunge, using a script by Bill Carter and starring Daniel Roebuck as Jay Leno, and John Michael Higgins as David Letterman. Helen Kushnick would be played by Kathy Bates, and Rich Little would do Johnny Carson. Ed Begley, Jr., was assigned to the cast, as was Treat Williams as Michael Ovitz.

The docudrama—it was basically seen as almost a comic takeoff on the higher levels of the television industry—aired in late February 1996, shown on HBO several nights in a row. The reviews were relatively good, with Howard Rosenberg of the *Los Angeles Times* describing it as an "endearing fracas," and most critics declaring it an amusing inside look at television.

The big joke, of course, was that the book's premise—that the NBC executives who had made the decision to go with Jay Leno over David Letterman had cost their network about $500 million by losing Letterman—was turned upside down in the months after the book appeared. By the time the docudrama was made, Leno had halted Letterman's two-year winning streak and moved into first place, where he remained. In addition, Leno won an Emmy in September 1995 for best variety program. And so the winner is . . .

The principals of the night-time talk-show battle certainly had a great deal to say about the way they appeared onscreen.

"From the pictures I've seen," Leno said, "they don't look like us or even real people as much as they do members of the Duracell family." He was referring to the shiny figures used in the battery commercials.

He went on. "I don't understand how such a simpleton [as Leno appeared in the film] could hold on to a major show for five years." He shrugged philosophically. "If I can't take it when they're making fun of me, I wouldn't be a very good sport."

Letterman called the whole thing "moronic" and noted that it was "the biggest waste of film since my wedding photos." And he wondered why the actor who played him had on a red wig. "Couldn't they get a picture or a piece of video?" he asked *Entertainment Tonight*. "It's not like I've been in the trunk of a car in Guatemala for the last fifteen years."

Letterman did declare he was grateful for not being represented the way his counterpart on NBC, Jay Leno, was. "Elephant man," he quipped.

When Leno picked up his Emmy at the Awards Banquet, he thanked everyone and then mentioned *The Late Shift* movie. "I guess they're going to have to change the ending of that movie."

As for Letterman, one of his latest lists—Top Ten Insults for Dave Letterman—read: "Letterman, let's face it—you put the 'suck' in success."

What they did at the end of *The Late Shift* was to add in paragraphs of information, pointing out that Letterman had won ninety weeks of ratings against Leno until July 1995, after which Leno had topped him and had won all the rest up to the present time.

And so the basic hero of the book by Bill Carter, David Letterman, turned out to be the goat of the docudrama, even though he was not portrayed that way.

Ah, show business!

It was during the Leno-Letterman ratings war that what Leno called "the worst week of my life" occurred—the week during which his eighty-two-year-old mother died of cancer. He had moved her and Angelo, his father, also eighty-two, from Andover to Florida, hoping the warm weather would benefit them. Several weeks later, the inevitable happened. His mother's health deteriorated.

"It was rough," Leno told viewers during his July 5, 1993, monologue. "From January to June, Mom was so sick." The Florida weather did not help matters. "I was talking to doctors on the phone every day, lining up nurses and all that stuff, at the same time trying to write a show. Sometimes during commercials I'd be making phone calls, making sure everything was all right."

Disliking Florida, Leno's mother and father moved back to Andover. Leno flew there on weekends to visit them. It was during one of these flights that his mother died after surgery.

In his monologue on July 5, he said in tribute to her, his voice choking back emotion:

"I count among my friends people like Jerry Seinfeld, George Carlin, Johnny Carson, and comedians David Letterman, Carol Burnett. But, you know, none of them could make me laugh the way she did. I really did lose the best friend I ever had."

About his mother Leno said, "We'd have these discussions where everything would be mixed up and turned around." When his picture appeared on the cover of *Time* magazine in 1992, she insisted it was only for the Massachusetts edition, saying, "They put you on the cover in our area because they knew you're from here."

Leno is proud and pleased his mother lived long enough to see his ascent to the top of the comedy scene. "My biggest fear was always that something would happen to my parents before I even got a chance to establish myself. My mom got to see me at Carnegie Hall and Vegas."

She liked it when he ribbed her in his routines. "Every time he pokes fun, that means he's thinking of me."

About a year later, in August 1994, Angelo Leno also died of cancer. Leno has nothing but fond memories of his father, Angelo. "I didn't know anything about show business, but I liked the part when you go to peoples' houses and tell them a funny story and keep them occupied. When I was a kid, my dad was always the guy at the convention who would be asked to give a funny talk before introducing the vice president of sales. Looked like fun. I used to like watching my dad do that. I said, I could do that, I bet."

Leno praised his father in a monologue the week after Angelo's death. His demeanor calm, Leno said, "I don't know. . . . It's a shame when you do this every day. . . . You write jokes . . . and things happen in life. I'd thought I'd take a minute to sort of talk about them. . . . I just thought I would tell you a little bit about my dad, if I could."

Leno stated that Angelo "didn't really have much reason to go on once my mom went. Fifty-seven years they were married."

Leno termed Angelo a "street kid" growing up in New York City. "Son of immigrant parents. I never knew how far my dad got in school. He would never tell me. I knew he quit somewhere. I don't know whether it was junior high or high school. He was a prize fighter and a truck driver and a mechanic. He went on to become an insurance salesman, and then he became a district manager and then went back to school and . . . a real up-by-the-bootstraps kind of guy."

Maybe Leno learned political correctness from Angelo, for he never heard Angelo "say a cross word to my mom, never saw him raise his hand. Never saw him drunk." He never heard Angelo pronounce an "ethnic slur."

Leno's homily proceeded. "There are people who go through life . . . and you know they write letters and they march and they do those things, which is great. And there are people who just do the right thing. For whatever reason, they don't ask for any reward." Such a person was Angelo.

At this point in his monologue, Leno's voice caught for the first time. He related that "nobody was brought up righter than I was."

With the death of his father, Leno now understood the meaning of the phrase "lonely at the top." His parents "were always there for me to talk to. Even two years ago, when we were going through, 'Oh, is Jay going to get fired? Is he going to be replaced?' my dad would always say, 'Hey, you fight the good fight, son. You just get in there and fight the good fight!'

"You know, it really is lonely at the top. You have no idea." Leno gasped, trying to draw a deep breath. "But . . . we'll fight the good fight, Pop."

Aside from these personal tragedies, actually, everything seemed to be coming up roses for Jay Leno. From the week of July 10–14 in 1995, *The Tonight Show* suddenly emerged as a first-time winner in the ratings battle between *Tonight* and *Late Show*. The ratings were tied for a bit, but then *The Tonight Show* emerged once again as the winner, and continued in that fashion right up through the rest of 1995 and on into 1996.

In the long run, though, another tiny battle of some significance was played out between the two comedians. Leno had opted to joke openly about happenings at the O. J. Simpson trial; Letterman had opted not to mention it at all.

Many in the industry cited that one factor—the O. J. Simpson stuff that Leno dared to use—as the chief reason for the reversal in the ratings.

It helped Leno's wallet as well—as if his wallet *needed* any help.

NBC inked a contract with Leno in December 1995 that was said to be between $11 million and $14 million—close to David Letterman's reported income at CBS: $14.5 million a year. The contract, incidentally, had a five-year run, which gave Leno security through the year 2000. Leno wanted to perform fifty-two weeks of the year, but NBC made him take four or five weeks off. Not a bad contract for a guy who used to wash cars for free to see if the boss would eventually notice him and hire him.

Things were indeed going up, up, and up. Plus vacation time! Exciting for Leno? Sure, except for the vacation part. "I come to work, and everybody applauds. My life's a vacation."

During this Indian summer of Leno's, another misunderstanding of sorts—that between Jay and Arsenio Hall—was patched up one night on Leno's show. In February 1996 the basketball star Magic Johnson, who had retired from the game some years before after being diagnosed HIV-positive, unretired himself to rejoin the Los Angeles Lakers. He then retired again some months later.

When he appeared on *The Tonight Show*, Leno noticed that he did not arrive alone, but was accompanied by Arsenio Hall, who no longer had his syndicated show, having called it quits some months before. Jay prevailed on Hall to appear before the audience during a commercial break—with the audience breaking out into Arsenio's "hoo hoo" cheer, while pumping their arms madly.

The brief meeting smoothed any ruffled feelings, and it appeared that the whole feud was simply a series of coincidences. First, Arsenio had used it as a ploy to get some newspaper space. Second, Jay had reasoned it out that way. Later, the bookings war had made it look as if *that* was the reason for the feud.

And so on and so forth.

In the end, Arsenio promised to appear on Leno's show on the day he had something important to promote.

The reversal of fortune between Leno's *Tonight Show* and Letterman's *Late Show* was attributed by observers of the television scene to a number of special factors. These included:

1. Shrewd adjustments made in the show by Leno.
    A. The new set.
    B. Substitution of Eubanks for Marsalis.
2. Leno's relentlessness in performing.
3. The precipitous drop of CBS in network standings.
4. Fallout from David Letterman's performance as host of the Oscar broadcast.

Leno's adjustments have been discussed, in particular the two main ones: the brand new set that put Leno in touch with his audience once again, and the departure of Branford Marsalis and the emergence of Kevin Eubanks as Leno's second banana.

Leno's relentlessness was a thing born unto him, in his genes, as it were. He had been brought up in a home that understood and lived by the work ethic. Why shouldn't he be a terribly apt student of competition?

The precipitous demise of CBS in the industry has already been discussed.

David Letterman's stint as emcee for the Academy Awards in Hollywood was not considered a success; it was pointed out that his failure made it much more acceptable to pan him as a star.

"I love this," Leno said. "I don't love it because of beating somebody else. Even before I had the show, I always loved going out on the road and working. Now the road is coming to my house. I feel like the old Danny Thomas show. Remember, he would be home and say, 'O.K. I'm going down to the club.' I loved that. That's how I feel now. I'm at home and then I can go down to my club."

To sum it up briefly:

"I just like working. With me, it's not ambition. It's effort. I'm not as good, but I'll stick with it."